Henry Fielding's
TOM JONES

ANTHONY J. HASSALL
Senior Lecturer in English
University of Newcastle

SYDNEY UNIVERSITY PRESS

SYDNEY UNIVERSITY PRESS
Press Building, University of Sydney

UNITED KINGDOM, EUROPE, MIDDLE EAST, AFRICA
International Scholarly Book Services (Europe)
Letchworth, England

NORTH AND SOUTH AMERICA
International Scholarly Book Services, Inc.
Forest Grove, Oregon

National Library of Australia Cataloguing-in-Publication data

Hassall, A. J.
Fielding's 'Tom Jones'.

(Sydney studies in literature)
Bibliography
ISBN 0 424 00054 7

1. Fielding, Henry, 1707–1754. Tom Jones.
I. Fielding, Henry, 1707–1754. Tom Jones. II. Title.
III. Title: Tom Jones. (Series)

823'.5

First published 1979
© Anthony J. Hassall 1979

Photosetting by Thomson Press (India) Limited, New Delhi
Printed in Australia by Macarthur Press (Books) Pty Limited, Parramatta

CONTENTS

Acknowledgements	vii
Introduction	ix
I Chapter One	1
II Chapter Two	46
III Chapter Three	81
Select Bibliography	113

For Loretta

ACKNOWLEDGEMENTS

A good many people have contributed in one way or another to the writing of this book. A grant of Study Leave from my own University, and the hospitality of Professor G. A. Wilkes and the English Studies Research Centre at Sydney University enabled me to work on it uninterruptedly. Professor Henry Knight Miller and Professor Martin C. Battestin generously shared their Fielding scholarship with me during my all too brief visits to their Universities. I would also like to thank Professor Ian Donaldson, who has encouraged my work on Fielding over a number of years, Dr Dianne Osland, who read the manuscript, and Mrs Marie Hill, who prepared it.

I am particularly indebted to Dr Doug Muecke for his reading of the manuscript, and for his advice and guidance over many years; and to Professor John Burrows for his generous support of the project at every stage, and for his critical reading of the manuscript. My greatest debt is to my wife, to whom the book is dedicated.

University of Newcastle   A. J. H.
March 1979

Introduction

In the Preface to *Joseph Andrews* Fielding describes the new form of fiction he had created in that work, and was to perfect in *Tom Jones*, as 'comic Epic-Poem in Prose'. The term 'poem', which has customarily been ignored as a synonym for 'epic', or as a seeming contradiction of 'prose', is I believe a positive component of Fielding's definition which works in creative tension with 'prose'—the phrase may serve as a first example of the density of Fielding's writing—and *Tom Jones* needs to be read more like an epic poem which celebrates unforgettably the wisdom of a culture, and less like a rough draft for a nineteenth-century novel. It is my contention that *Tom Jones* requires and generously repays close and detailed reading of the kind too often reserved for the verse epic which preceded it, or the Jamesian novel which followed. That it is a comic epic partly explains why it has not received such attention until fairly recently. One of the funniest and most enjoyable of English classics, it has never lacked readers, but there has been a reluctance to accept that so humorously entertaining a work could also be as serious as *Paradise Lost*. Homer's comic epic the *Margites* has not survived, and critics do not have a model for the comic epic with the sanction of antiquity. Cervantes' *Don Quixote*, which Fielding said he was imitating in *Joseph Andrews*, has had to serve. It is allowed to be both comic and serious, even indeed profound; but Fielding, who is funnier, has found it harder to be taken seriously. 'Surely a Man may speak Truth with a smiling Countenance',[1] he argues, anticipating the difficulty. Aware like Cervantes that the clichés and truisms of conventional thought are inadequate and often hypocritical,

---

[1] Martin C. Battestin and Fredson Bowers (eds), *Tom Jones*, Wesleyan University Press [1977], XI, i; p. 569. All quotations are taken from this revised Wesleyan edition. Subsequent references are included in the text. Quotations from *Joseph Andrews* are also from the Wesleyan edition, Martin C. Battestin (ed.), Oxford 1967.

Fielding treats them comically to alert the reader to the limited moral awareness they signal, and to prompt the search for a truer awareness than they allow. He sees no danger that genuine values will be compromised along with false ones: 'I defy', says Joseph Andrews, 'the wisest Man in the World to turn a true good Action into Ridicule' (III, vi; 234). Not all of Fielding's critics have been persuaded, however, and despite his insistence that the comedy is essential to his moral purpose it has too often been assumed that a book as amusing as *Tom Jones* must lack that high seriousness that Matthew Arnold held to be the distinguishing feature of the highest art.

It is not, therefore, surprising that the critical esteem in which *Tom Jones* has been held has fluctuated considerably. While there have been influential critics from Dr Johnson to Dr Leavis who have condemned or dismissed it, there have also been critics from Coleridge to the present who have lauded it enthusiastically as 'among the supreme achievements of the world's literary art'.[2] In recent decades *Tom Jones* has been subjected to intense critical scrutiny, and has emerged with its reputation considerably enhanced. The myth of hearty Harry Fielding, who loved a wench and a bottle, and who dashed off brilliant, libertine pieces in his spare time, proved, because of its very Byronic colourfulness, difficult to gainsay, despite extensive scholarly refutation from the time of Wilbur L. Cross's biography (1918) to the present.[3] Ford Madox Ford puts it at its most extravagant:

> fellows like Fielding, and to some extent Thackeray, who pretend that if you are a gay drunkard, lecher, squanderer of your goods and fumbler in placket-holes you will eventually find a benevolent uncle, concealed father or benefactor who will shower on you bags of tens of thousands of guineas, estates and the hands of adorable mistresses—those fellows are dangers to the body-politic and horribly bad constructors of plots.[4]

---

[2] Henry Knight Miller, *Henry Fielding's 'Tom Jones' and the Romance Tradition*, University of Victoria, B.C. 1976, p. 101. For the history of Fielding criticism see Frederic T. Blanchard, *Fielding the Novelist: A Study in Historical Criticism*, New Haven 1926; and Ronald Paulson and Thomas Lockwood (eds), *Henry Fielding: The Critical Heritage*, London 1969. There are excellent accounts of criticism hostile to Fielding in Robert Alter, *Fielding and the Nature of the Novel*, Cambridge, Mass. 1968, pp. 3–25; and Bernard Harrison, *Henry Fielding's Tom Jones: The Novelist as Moral Philosopher*, London 1975, pp. 11–27.

[3] *The History of Henry Fielding*, 3 vols, New Haven 1918.

[4] *The English Novel*, London 1929, pp. 99–100.

If, in these enlightened times, there are still readers of *Tom Jones* who find any similarity between this description and what happens in the book, then they are out of step with the impressive reassessment of Fielding effected in recent years, culminating in Martin C. Battestin's forthright statement that: '*Tom Jones* is at once the last and the consummate literary achievement of England's Augustan age'.[5] The present study is built on this new body of criticism. It views *Tom Jones* as at once very funny and entirely serious, as comic not only in the sense of producing laughter, and ending happily, but also in the sense of reflecting a world presided over by a benevolent providence. Its comedy is divine, like Dante's, as well as human, as Fielding insists comedy should be in the Preface to *Joseph Andrews*. I am convinced that the more closely the book is read the more apparent it becomes that it is a work of far-reaching human sympathy, real moral subtlety, and marked artistic originality.

The origins of *Tom Jones*, like those of its hero, are the subject of some uncertainty: we have little definite information, and can only speculate on how so major a work came to be written when it did.[6] By the time he began work on it, probably early in 1745, Fielding must have seemed to many of his contemporaries no more than the hackney writer that, as an indigent young man of twenty-two in search of a living, he had said he would have to become. For fifteen years he had been writing plays, poems, essays, journalism, political pamphlets, and prose fiction, with very varied and occasionally spectacular success, but he had never settled into one mould or made one form or genre his own, and, with the exception of *Joseph Andrews*, which showed him what he could do, he had written no major work. He had tried hardest for success on the stage. He spent a turbulent eight years (1730–7) writing for and eventually managing a theatrical company in London in the lively decade immediately preceding the great age of Garrick. He made a precocious entry as a dramatist in 1728 when, at the age of twenty-one, he had *Love in Several Masques* produced at Drury Lane, and he made an even more spectacular exit in 1737 when his biting political satire prompted Walpole to pass the Licensing Act which ended his career as a dramatist. In the intervening years he had written a string of brilliant but evanescent farces, some good ballad-operas, and some second-rate comedies.

---

[5] *Twentieth Century Interpretations of Tom Jones*, Englewood Cliffs, N.J. 1968, p. 1.
[6] The best account of the composition of *Tom Jones* is Martin C. Battestin's in the two-volume Wesleyan edition of the novel, Oxford 1974, Vol. 1, pp. xix–xlii. What follows is indebted to this account.

Fielding himself valued the comedies, upon which he lavished some care, but his audiences preferred the satiric farces and the rollicking ballad-operas. He was never a sure judge of the success of his own work. By 1744, after more occasional writing, and further restless experimentation, he seemed ready to give up literature altogether, and settle for a legal career. 'There is not', he writes, 'I believe, (and it is bold to affirm), a single free Briton in this kingdom who hates his wife more heartily than I detest the Muses.'[7] In his *Miscellanies* (1743) he had brought together what remained unpublished of his work, and in the preface he had announced that he would publish no more anonymous work. His political friends were still in opposition to the government which had banned him from the stage. It may well have seemed an opportune time to put an end to a literary career that had been, to say the least, unevenly rewarding.

His personal circumstances at the time were also less than propitious. In November 1744 his ten-year marriage to his beloved Charlotte had ended with her death. It was the last and most severe of a series of misfortunes, personal and financial, which made the period from 1741–4 a particularly difficult one for Fielding. He writes, for example, of the winter of 1741–2, that he was 'laid up in the Gout, with a favourite Child dying in one Bed, and my Wife in a Condition very little better, on another, attended with other Circumstances, which served as very proper Decorations to such a Scene', and he apologizes for any resulting 'Faults' in his *Miscellanies*.[8] In the month following his wife's death, in November 1744, however, Fielding's fortunes began to turn. His political friends and patrons—most notably George Lyttleton, to whom *Tom Jones* is dedicated—at last came to power in the 'Broad-Bottom' government. No doubt it was small comfort at the time, but their accession to power opened up the possibility of more extended literary patronage, and an eventual legal appointment which would confer some security on Fielding and his family. Their patronage was limited, and Fielding was obliged to earn it by writing in support of the government when occasion demanded, which it all too often did, interrupting the work on *Tom Jones* which was now begun; but it is doubtful whether he would have felt the confidence to undertake so large a project, and to persevere with it, had his friends not encouraged him as they did. As for his wife, his monument to her was to be the glowing portrayal of Sophia in his masterpiece. It was

---

[7] William E. Henley (ed.), *The Complete Works of Henry Fielding, Esq.*, 16 vols, London 1903, Vol. XVI, p. 8. Hereafter cited as Henley.

[8] Henry Knight Miller (ed.), *Miscellanies by Henry Fielding, Esq; Volume One*, Oxford 1972, p. 14.

a noble celebration of 'one from whom', he had said, 'I draw all the solid Comfort of my Life';[9] but if Fielding praised her generously, he did not entirely pine away after her death. In November 1747, when *Tom Jones* was well advanced, Fielding married his wife's maid Mary Daniel, then six months pregnant with his son William. It was a courageous if socially ignominious acknowledgement of their relationship, which led his cousin Lady Mary Wortley Montagu to write of his 'rapture with his cook-maid'.[10] He had ridiculed such marriages six years earlier in *Shamela*, and it is a measure of the man that that did not deter him.

The major public event to interrupt the writing of *Tom Jones* was the Jacobite rebellion of 1745. Fielding wrote energetically in support of the Hanoverian cause in *The True Patriot* (1745-6), *The Jacobite's Journal* (1747-8), and in a number of fugitive political pamphlets. The rebellion was also worked into the novel, which perhaps accounts, as Martin C. Battestin has suggested, for the five-month lapse of chronology in Book Five, as well as for the Jacobite sympathies of Western and Partridge, and Tom's staunch support of the Protestant cause.[11] Despite these stirring events, with their demands on Fielding's time and pen, and despite the legal work to which he devoted himself, he found in the years 1745-8 those 'Thousands of Hours' (XI, i; 571) which went into the composition of *Tom Jones*. It was an opportunity that was not to be repeated. In July 1748 Fielding was appointed magistrate for Westminster. His maternal grandfather Sir Henry Gould had been a judge of the Queen's Bench, and Fielding was to be a distinguished magistrate; indeed his devotion to duty was such as to damage his health, and to interfere with further creative writing. *Amelia* (1751) did not repeat the triumph of *Tom Jones*, though Fielding himself thought highly of it. Just why the years 1745-8 proved conducive to creative work of the highest order we shall probably never know. Arthur Murphy, Fielding's collaborator and first biographer, speaks of 'the second grand epoch of Mr. Fielding's genius, when all his faculties were in perfect unison, and conspired to produce a complete work';[12] but even he, who might have known, does not explain why this period produced so sustained a burst of creative energy from a man who had so recently, and so vehemently forsworn the Muses.

Whatever the cause, the result was an unpredictably spectacular

---

[9] Ibid., p. 13.
[10] Paulson and Lockwood (eds), *Henry Fielding: The Critical Heritage*, p. 394. Other reactions to the marriage are described in: Henry Fielding, *The Jacobite's Journal and Related Writings*, ed. W. B. Coley, Oxford 1974, pp. lxxx-lxxxi.
[11] *Tom Jones*, Vol. I, p. xxxix.
[12] Paulson and Lockwood (eds), *Henry Fielding: The Critical Heritage*, p. 424.

success, and on a scale larger than Fielding had previously attempted. In *Eurydice Hissed* (1737), he describes the youthful inspiration which enabled him 'to write nine scenes with spirit in one day'.[13] Such happy fluency does not, however, produce one of 'the three most perfect plots ever planned', and Coleridge's praise of *Tom Jones* was earned, in part, by slow and painstaking construction, which produced, in time, a graceful and elegant book, proportioned in the Palladian manner.[14] Fielding was conscious that he was writing an epic, and he was Augustan enough to see in the epic the highest reach of the creative human spirit, a form which demanded of its practitioners meticulous attention to detail as well as grandeur of design and cultural commonality of theme.

There has been a good deal of critical debate about the design and the plotting of *Tom Jones*, but less attention has been paid, at least until recently, to the texture of the writing. One of the major aims of the present study is, as I have suggested, to look closely at the verbal fabric of the book. A second, related aim is to examine the way in which it articulates Fielding's very personal view of the relationship between art and life. Like much of the rest of his writing, *Tom Jones* is a resolutely self-conscious book, continually drawing attention to its own status as an artefact, and persistently disrupting the suspension of disbelief. This is not, I think, done from a suspicion of art of the kind expressed by Plato and Tolstoy.[15] Fielding sees art as a dangerous substitute for life only when it seeks, and is given, the wrong kind of credence; when it is believed as if it were indeed a substitute for life, or for a true perception of life. He would not agree with Joyce that: 'art is not an escape from life . . . art . . . is the very central expression of life'.[16] For Fielding art runs parallel to, but separate from life. If the two are confused, either for romantic escapism, or to identify art as the best of life, then art is unable to fulfil its true function, which is to reflect and illuminate life in an artificial manner. There are, as I shall try to show, a number of scenes in *Tom Jones* devoted to the definition of this function of art. Fielding is not only telling his reader how to live, but how to use a work of art like *Tom Jones* to learn how to live.

Tom Jones is then more than the happy accident it must have seemed to Fielding's contemporaries, who knew his earlier, slighter work. It is also more than the happy-go-lucky, roistering celebration of the pleasures of

---

[13] William W. Appleton (ed.), *The Historical Register For the Year 1736 and Eurydice Hissed*, London 1968, p. 64.

[14] Blanchard, *Fielding the Novelist*, p. 321.

[15] See *The Republic of Plato*, trans. F. M. Cornford, Oxford 1941, pp. 78–83 and pp. 316–32; and L. N. Tolstoy, *What Is Art?*, trans. A. Maude, New York 1960.

[16] James Joyce, *Stephen Hero*, London 1956, p. 90.

life that some of the more serious of its first readers, like Richardson and Johnson, took it to be, and condemned it for being. It has been much adapted, to stage, opera, and film, from the time it first appeared to our own time. Tony Richardson's film version (1964) admirably caught that aspect of the book that critics from Johnson to Ford Madox Ford deplore—its joy in the physical pleasures of life—but did less than justice to its high seriousness as a work of art and of the theory of art.[17] A much more successful, if altogether more modest adaptation was a serialized radio reading of the book in daily ten-minute segments. This left Fielding's writing essentially intact, and it emphasized how much was to be gained from reading the book slowly, stopping after each episode, and reflecting on its meaning and significance. The process was illuminating, and Fielding's advice to the reader that that was how his book ought to be read was entirely vindicated. *Tom Jones* has been a much-read and a much-loved book for more than two hundred years. It has not, however, always been a wisely-read book, and I think there are still riches to be recovered from reading it as Fielding wanted it to be read. That is what I shall attempt to do in the following pages.

---

[17] John Osborne, *Tom Jones: A Film Script*, London 1964.

Chapter One

In the first six books of *Tom Jones*, with which this chapter will be concerned, Fielding presents his history of Tom's early life at Paradise Hall in Somerset, and begins to educate the reader into the meaning of his work. In the Dedication to his friend and patron George Lyttleton he provides an early clue to that meaning. His purpose is, he says, to display with all the wit and humour of which he is master 'that Beauty of Virtue which may attract the Admiration of Mankind', and to convince men of 'that solid inward Comfort of Mind' (7) which accompanies its possession. Within the text proper he is less sober and more equivocal about his purpose, as we shall see, believing, with Shaftesbury, that high seriousness is effective only when it is unassuming and unobtrusive.[1] But in the Dedication he lays his masks aside and tells us directly what he is about, and the touchstone which he thus provides, and invites us to use to measure the success of his 'good Attempt' (8), is therefore well worth bearing in mind as we begin to read *Tom Jones*. In the description of Tom's early life we see the tangle of vice and virtue that we encounter in the world. Tom has to learn to distinguish between the two in others and in himself. The education of the reader, who observes this learning process and is also addressed directly in the author's commentary, is parallel to, interwoven with, yet separate from that of Tom. It is the reader who is ultimately to be persuaded that virtue alone brings that comfort of mind which is the nearest thing to happiness in this life, a persuasion to be made as pleasurable as possible by the use of an engaging hero, a lively narrative, and a commentary full of wit and humour.

Having offered the reader a brief and succinct outline of his purpose, Fielding hastens into the midst of his story, and though he is a talkative

[1] See 'Advice to an Author' in John M. Robertson (ed.), *Characteristics*, New York 1964, pp. 103–4.

author he does not fill up his pages by repeating his text at the end of every paragraph (XII, viii; 652). His subsequent statements of overall purpose are few and indirect: he tackles issues as they arise from events in the narrative, and the major ideas, characters, and themes are treated differently in different contexts. This makes it unsatisfactory to generalize from one, or even from a number of such contexts, since all of them need to be taken into account as contributing something to the total picture. In any case generalizations about Fielding's thought do less than justice to the richness of the book. The quality of his writing does not reside in any abstractable content or doctrine, which usually ends up looking commonplace and unremarkable,[2] but in the realization of moral issues in specific narrative situations and, more importantly, in the author's local rhetoric. It is the density of texture of this local writing, and the development of a series of closely-written scenes which are different but related, which give Fielding's work its life, its wit, and its moral subtlety. I intend to follow Fielding's practice in this study and to consider issues as they arise.

The place to begin, therefore, is at the beginning. The first words of *Tom Jones* are 'An Author', and the first introductory chapter opens with a characterization of the author, and with a sophisticated play upon the author-reader relationship, both of which are to be more fully portrayed and discussed than is usual in fiction. Joyce, one of the few novelists to have imitated Fielding at all closely, describes what he calls the 'epic' relationship between the artist and his work in *A Portrait of the Artist as a Young Man*: 'the personality of the artist passes into the narration itself, flowing round and round the persons and the action like a vital sea'.[3] Fielding uses a culinary rather than a uterine image to describe this relationship, but his meaning is similar: 'the Excellence of the mental Entertainment consists less in the Subject, than in the Author's Skill in well dressing it up' (I, i; 33). In choosing to give such prominence to the author Fielding may seem to be looking back to the epic rather than forward to the novel, but in fact many novelists have followed Fielding and Cervantes rather than Flaubert and James and have placed the author within the novel and not god-like and uninvolved above it all. While Joyce, Flaubert's disciple, excludes the character of the author

---

[2] Two exceptions to this general rule are Henry Knight Miller, *Essays on Fielding's Miscellanies: A Commentary on Volume One*, Princeton 1961; and Harrison, *Henry Fielding's Tom Jones*.

[3] James Joyce, *A Portrait of the Artist as a Young Man*, London 1956, p. 219.

from his fiction yet retains a maze of styles to indicate his existence, other novelists testify to the continued presence of authorial character. The author in Butler's *The Way of All Flesh*, for example, writes:

> I know that whether I like it or no I am portraying myself more surely than I am portraying any of the characters whom I set before the reader.[4]

And L. P. Hartley comes even closer to Fielding: 'in even the most austere novels there is generally a kind of flirtation between the author and his reader'.[5] Fielding has no need for such half-apologetic admissions, however, and embraces enthusiastically the opportunity for authorial characterization in the first chapter of his epic. His author is the host of an Ordinary, an eating-house open to the public, and the readers are the patrons, who will come and go as they find the fare to their taste or not. One immediate effect of this choice of image is to bring the author and the reader face-to-face as it were, to re-establish the oral tradition of the first epics and, in England, of Chaucer in particular. Bertrand Bronson sees this as a very personal relationship: 'we feel that we know him [Fielding] better, and more intimately, on his own chosen terms, than anyone else to whom we are introduced'.[6] The author presents his book to the reader like a host regaling his clients with an anecdote. It is a down-to-earth analogy, commonplace and yet unexpected. It is to be an eating book, like 'that eating Poem of the Odyssey' (IX, v; 509), an unromantically physical book, presided over by a shrewd and jovial host who knows the manners of men at table, where appetites demand satisfaction and where, as Joyce pointed out in the 'Lestrygonians' episode of *Ulysses*, the scene is often not a pretty one.

The tone, however, is less satiric than in Fielding's other work, and more comic. The host is affable, deferential without subservience, knowing, genial, and amused. This is not to say there is not a tension inherent in the host-client relationship, or in the author-reader relationship, but while it is admitted that the clients or the readers 'will challenge a Right to censure, to abuse, and to d--n their Dinner without Controul', the host or author maintains an unruffled politeness. He is not, however, imperceptive: there are a good many inn-keepers later in the novel, and to a man (or woman) they pride themselves on their ability to

---

[4] London 1958, p. 61.
[5] *The Novelist's Responsibility*, London 1967, p. 3.
[6] *Facets of the Enlightenment*, Berkeley and Los Angeles 1968, p. 315.

place their guests precisely on society's ladder and to treat them accordingly. The task for an author is not so easy:

> Reader, it is impossible we should know what Sort of Person thou wilt be: For, perhaps, thou may'st be as learned in Human Nature as *Shakespear* himself was, and, perhaps, thou may'st be no wiser than some of his Editors. (X, i; 523)

But, like a prudent host, the author endeavours to accommodate his critics according to their taste and worth. As he keeps a public ordinary, at which all persons are welcome for their money, he cannot hope that all who come will bring a discriminating taste; but he can endeavour to keep the more boorish clients in their place, while treating his more perceptive readers with courtesy, and guiding them through the many courses offered to the most delectable morsels and the specialities of the house. All this is done in a tone of comic buoyancy, of easy, assured, even playful mastery which inspires the book from beginning to end to a degree unmatched in Fielding's other work. *Tom Jones* is a work of pure comedy, in which the shadows cast, while providing the complications necessary for a plot reflecting the inevitably mixed and often unhappy human lot, are lightened ultimately for the protagonists by the author's providential care. Claude Rawson writes perceptively of Fielding's rendering of the dark underside of the Augustan vision in *Henry Fielding and the Augustan Ideal under Stress*, but in doing so his emphasis rightly falls on works like *Jonathan Wild* and *Amelia*.[7] *Tom Jones* is Fielding's sunniest book, and since his talent, at its highest reach, is comic rather than satiric it is also his best, superior to the monochromatic division of vice and virtue in *Jonathan Wild*, and to the troubled mixture of comic and satiric tones in *Amelia*.

With the subject thus announced, the author introduced, and the comic tone established, the history of Tom Jones begins. The family which is to surround Tom is representative of the world in which he will have to learn how to live. Mr Allworthy is the centre. Confronted with a sleeping infant on his return from London, he responds with characteristic generosity, deciding to raise the child in his own house. But if he has a 'Heart that hungers after Goodness' (I, iii; 41), those around him are less nobly motivated. Bridget Allworthy, Tom's mother, plays the hypocrite with such skill that she not only escapes the strictures of a censorious world for her lapse with Tom's father, but she is able to manipulate her brother's

[7] London 1972.

good-nature so that the boy is virtually raised as her own. If Tom's generous spirit is derived from his uncle, and perhaps his father, Master Blifil's prudence clearly comes from his mother. The outside world may be represented by Mrs Deborah Wilkins, whose rapidly changing responses to the situation are a study in themselves. Urgently summoned by Mr Allworthy, she spends a good deal of time adjusting her hair before proceeding to his room:

> She therefore no sooner opened the Door, and saw her Master standing by the Bedside in his Shirt, with a Candle in his Hand, than she started back in a most terrible Fright, and might perhaps have swooned away, had he not now recollected his being undrest, and put an End to her Terrors, by desiring her to stay without the Door till he had thrown some Cloaths over his Back, and was become incapable of shocking the pure Eyes of Mrs. *Deborah Wilkins*, who, tho' in the 52d Year of her Age, vowed she had never beheld a Man without his Coat. Sneerers and prophane Wits may perhaps laugh at her first Fright, yet my graver Reader, when he considers the Time of Night, the Summons from her Bed, and the Situation in which she found her Master, will highly justify and applaud her Conduct; unless the Prudence, which must be supposed to attend Maidens at that Period of Life at which Mrs. *Deborah* had arrived, should a little lessen his Admiration. (I, iii; 39–40)

The most interesting thing about this long comment is the choice of alternative responses suggested to the reader, who may be grave or profane, who may laugh at the 'modesty' of Mrs Deborah, applaud her circumspection or censure her want of judgement, or indeed combine any or all of these. Far from clarifying the reader's response, the commentary here complicates it. Comedy there certainly is in Mrs Deborah's misjudging of Allworthy, but the finer points of moral interpretation are by no means resolved. In the next chapter, the author says:

> Reader, take care, I have unadvisedly led thee to the Top of as high a Hill as Mr. *Allworthy's*, and how to get thee down without breaking thy Neck, I do not well know. (I, iv; 43–4)

The reader does need to take care if he is to read this book aright. Mrs Wilkins's fright is a simple example; but there are more complex ones to come.

When she recovers from her fear or hope of a sexual advance from Allworthy—which shows her to be 'prudent' in the worldly sense but stupidly imperceptive of her employer's character—and when she sees the sleeping infant, she rightly warns her master that if he provides for it it will be assumed to be his own. Warming to her theme of the ways of the world, she advises leaving the child at the church-warden's door where, 'it is two to one but it lives till it is found in the Morning' (I, iii; 41). Allworthy ignores this brutal advice, and she is obliged to remember that she enjoys a 'most excellent Place' in his employ and to care for the child as she is instructed. When her mistress is informed the next morning that the child is to be raised in the household, Mrs Deborah expects an eruption of outraged virtue, and when this is not forthcoming in Allworthy's presence, she expects it all the more vehemently behind his back, though she prudently waits her cue from Mrs Bridget, who surprises her by raising only a token objection to Allworthy's plan. Having endured so many enforced amendments to her natural feelings and expectations, she vents her displeasure by descending upon the village, 'to insult and tyrannize over little People' (I, vi; 47), in pursuit of the supposed mother of Tom.

It is clear that Tom has come into a morally chequered world, and that he is fortunate to enjoy the protection of a generous and well-intentioned uncle, and to profit from the machinations of a mother who protects him without owning him. Without these powerful patrons, Tom may well not have survived that first night at the church-warden's door. Even with them he is far from secure, as 'it was the universal Opinion of all Mr. *Allworthy's* Family, that he was certainly born to be hanged' (III, ii; 118). The moral isolation of Tom's uncle in the midst of a family and neighbours who are cynical and imperceptive is clearly indicated when he is first introduced to the reader. The author's account of Allworthy's marriage shows both how devoted a husband he was, and how few there were to appreciate him:

> This Gentleman had, in his Youth, married a very worthy and beautiful Woman, of whom he had been extremely fond: By her he had three Children, all of whom died in their Infancy. He had likewise had the Misfortune of burying this beloved Wife herself, about five Years before the Time in which this History chuses to set out. This Loss, however great, he bore like a Man of Sense and Constancy; tho' it must be confest, he would often talk a little whimsically on this Head: For he sometimes said, he looked on himself as still married, and considered his Wife as only gone a little before him, a Journey which he should most certainly, sooner or later, take after her; and that he had not the least Doubt of meeting her again, in a Place where he should never part with her more. Sentiments for which his Sense was

arraigned by one Part of his Neighbours, his Religion by a second, and his Sincerity by a third. (I, ii; 35)

The abrupt triple assault in the final sentence on Allworthy's amiable fondness for his dead wife, which has been lingered over sympathetically by the author, confronts the reader with the chasm between Allworthy's generous affections and his neighbours' nasty and suspicious minds. If those same neighbours think that Tom was born to be hanged, he cannot be all bad.

In the very next paragraph the author adopts a different method to introduce Bridget Allworthy to the reader.[8] She has none of the quixotic fancies which leave her brother open to misinterpretation by his neighbours. On the contrary she and her neighbours understand one another very well:

> This Lady was now somewhat past the Age of 30, an Æra, at which, in the Opinion of the malicious, the Title of Old Maid may, with no Impropriety, be assumed. She was of that Species of Women, whom you commend rather for good Qualities than Beauty, and who are generally called by their own Sex, very good Sort of Women—as good a Sort of Woman, Madam, as you would wish to know. (I, ii; 35–6)

In presenting her as she appears to society—the worst that neighbourly malice can do is to call her an old maid—the author indicates that her character is governed by social appearances not principles. Her acceptance as a good sort of woman by the neighbours who are sceptical about her brother is both a comment on her and a comment on them. When Jane Austen begins *Mansfield Park* with society's view of the marriages of the three Ward sisters, the effect is to suggest that the sisters share their society's crudely materialistic view of marriage, and are as little interested in personal affection in their own marriages as an outside observer. Bridget is similarly characterized by the way she is presented. When the author turns to describing her opinions he chooses her prudence as characteristic: that prudence which protects her from imagined sexual approaches:

> I have observed (tho' it may seem unaccountable to the Reader) that this Guard of Prudence, like the Trained Bands, is always readiest to go on Duty where there is the least Danger. (37)

---

[8] On Bridget's function in the book see Sheridan Baker, 'Bridget Allworthy: The Creative Pressures of Fielding's Plot', *Papers of the Michigan Academy of Science, Arts, and Letters*, Vol. LII, 1967, pp. 345–56.

So it proves with Bridget herself who despite her prudence is twice seduced. But if she is prone to lapses, she is prudence itself in managing the consequences: Tom is secured in her own family without suspicion falling on her, and Master Blifil's birth eight months after her marriage to Captain Blifil is explained away (II, ii; 78). Bridget is able to control appearances so that her violations of the social code escape notice.

Fielding's sustained exploration of the parallel sets of virtues and vices which go under the name of prudence, Bridget's defining characteristic, has been extensively treated in recent criticism.[9] A similar if more modest play is made with the various meanings of the adjective 'solid' in the opening chapters of *Tom Jones*, particularly those concerned with Bridget. The term first appears in the Dedication where, as we have seen, it is used in the most positive sense to describe: 'that solid inward Comfort of Mind, which is the sure Companion of Innocence and Virtue' (7). The term here means well founded or established, of real value or importance, and is used entirely unironically. When Allworthy is introduced in the second chapter he is said to have: 'an agreeable Person, a sound Constitution, a solid Understanding, and a benevolent Heart' (I, ii; 34). The description is complimentary— a solid understanding is one of sound, sober, and reliable judgement[10]—but the usage is less unequivocal than the previous one, and the events which follow demonstrate that Allworthy's understanding may be imposed upon, and that while he is steadily intelligent in weighing the evidence with which he is provided, he may be misled by false evidence because he lacks his creator's sharp eye for a rogue. Solid is, nonetheless, a term of strong approbation in these two contexts.

When Bridget surveys Captain Blifil as a potential husband there is a facetious description of his attributes which emphasizes his physical strength as his only admirable quality. Bridget, however, likes what she sees:

> Tho' Miss *Bridget* was a Woman of the greatest Delicacy of Taste; yet such were the Charms of the Captain's Conversation, that she totally overlooked the Defects of his Person. She imagined, and perhaps very wisely, that she should enjoy more agreeable Minutes with the Captain, than with a much prettier Fellow; and forewent the

---

[9] See Eleanor N. Hutchens, '"Prudence" in *Tom Jones*: A Study of Connotative Irony', *Philological Quarterly*, Vol. XXXIX, 1960, pp. 496–507; and Glenn W. Hatfield, *Henry Fielding and the Language of Irony*, Chicago 1968, pp. 179–96.

[10] The meanings are the relevant ones from the *Oxford English Dictionary*. In *Johnson's Dictionary* the relevant entries are: 'real; not empty; true; not fallacious'; and 'not light; not superficial; grave; profound'.

HENRY FIELDING'S
Tom Jones

SYDNEY STUDIES IN LITERATURE

FOUNDING EDITOR (1965-7): the late Professor K. G. W. Cross, then Head of the English Department, University of Newcastle

GENERAL EDITORS (1967-): G. A. Wilkes, Challis Professor of English Literature and Dr A. P. Riemer, Associate Professor of English Literature, University of Sydney

    HENRY FIELDING'S *TOM JONES*
        by Anthony J. Hassall
    JAMES JOYCE'S *ULYSSES* (*out of print*)
        by Clive Hart
    JANE AUSTEN'S *EMMA*
        by J. F. Burrows
    THE MAJOR POEMS OF JOHN KEATS
        by Norman Talbot
    MILTON'S *PARADISE LOST*
        by Michael Wilding
    THE POETRY OF ROBERT LOWELL
        by Vivian Smith
    A READING OF SHAKESPEARE'S *ANTONY AND CLEOPATRA*
        by A. P. Riemer
    SHAKESPEARE'S *HAMLET*
        by Derick R. Marsh

Consideration of pleasing her Eyes, in order to procure herself much more solid Satisfaction. (I, xi; 66)

The sexual innuendo detonated by 'solid' reverberates through the 'agreeable Minutes' Bridget imagines enjoying in 'conversation' with the Captain, and a close examination of the time scheme indicates that the couple's criminal conversation began as soon as they met, as is here hinted at in 'perhaps very wisely'. In addition to being funny, the joke exposes the rampant sexual appetite that Bridget almost succeeds in concealing behind an affectation of prudishness. 'Solid' is a discreet and proper word which Bridget herself might have chosen, and it reveals her true coarseness like a Freudian slip.

A paragraph later there is a further use of the term: 'The Captain likewise very wisely preferred the more solid Enjoyments he expected with this Lady, to the fleeting Charms of Person' (66–7). His solid enjoyments are financial not sexual, but he is as earnest for them as Bridget is for hers, and the two therefore quickly come to an understanding. The debased use of 'solid' in these contexts, paired with its elevated use to describe innocence and virtue, and Allworthy's understanding, illustrates Fielding's practice of exploring the potential of the language he uses. The reader is obliged to consider each usage in its context and to judge the meaning accordingly. Words, like characters, are by no means always what they seem.

The deceptiveness of appearances is dramatically illustrated in the search for Tom's parents which follows his discovery in Allworthy's bed. Mrs Wilkins descends on the village, is directed to Jenny Jones as a possible mother, and is surprised when the girl confesses. When she is taken before Mr Allworthy in his role as magistrate, instead of committing her to Bridewell he lectures her on the consequences of fornication and then arranges for her to start a new life away from the shame of her sin. She declines to name the supposed father, pleading 'the most religious Vows and Protestations' (I, vii; 54) she has undertaken to conceal his identity. On a first reading of the book the scene offers a plausible account of Tom's parentage. His mother is raised above the common by her 'very uncommon Share of Understanding' (I, vi; 48), and the mysterious, unnamed father is likely to be someone of distinction. Tom we feel sure will turn out to be no ordinary foundling. For the reader who has read the book before, and who knows the truth about Tom, the sequence is replete with carefully structured ironies. Jenny Jones is innocent, and Allworthy's rhetoric is misdirected. Despite his thoughtful and well-intentioned plan to prevent her first supposed lapse inevitably leading to others, she becomes a woman of comparatively easy virtue who eventually richly deserves the sermon she did not merit at the time she heard it. Bridget, who did merit it: 'sucked in . . . the instructive Lecture delivered by Mr. *Allworthy*' (I, viii; 55) at the key-hole of the study door. Neither Jenny nor Bridget, however, profit at all from the advice, since both go on to further indiscretions. Like other givers of good advice, Allworthy might have saved himself the trouble. In fact he is comprehensively duped by his sister and Jenny, though the author defends his perception as far as he can:

> The Ingenuity of this Behaviour, had gained *Jenny* so much Credit with this worthy Man, that he easily believed what she told him: For as she had disdained to excuse herself by a Lie, and had hazarded his farther Displeasure in her present Situation, rather than she would forefeit her Honour, or Integrity, by betraying another, he had but little Apprehension that she would be guilty of Falshood towards himself. (I, vii; 55)

Allworthy is no fool, but he is no match for the devious cunning of his sister. When Bridget later comes to an understanding with Captain Blifil, the lovers hypocritically feign indifference towards one another in front of Allworthy, who:

> must have had the Insight of the Devil (or perhaps some of his worse Qualities) to have entertained the least Suspicion of what was going forward. (I, xi; 69)

Allworthy's treatment of Jenny results, in a final irony, in 'the good Gossips of the Neighbourhood' (I, ix; 59) spreading slanderous accounts that Allworthy was lenient towards her because he was himself the father of her child, and that he had spirited her away 'with a Design too black to be mentioned' (59).

The lecture that Allworthy delivers to Jenny shines out like a good deed in the naughty world which surrounds it. What he has to say about love desiring the good of its object will be echoed by the author and by Tom in other deliberately unlikely contexts throughout *Tom Jones*, as we shall see. However inappropriate these contexts may make the sentiments appear, they nonetheless emerge uncompromised if often unappreciated by their immediate audience. These contrasts between a sentiment and its context are engineered by Fielding for comic and ironic effect, and to illustrate the common confusion of virtue and vice in the world.

As early as the second chapter of *Tom Jones* the author had served notice of his intention to: 'digress, through this whole History, as often as I see Occasion' (I, ii; 37). This intention is implemented in the commentary which generously accompanies the narrative, and in the introductory chapters prefixed to each of the eighteen books. The commentary, of which we have already seen examples, ranges from barely perceptible stylistic shading of incidents through interpretative commentary to direct dialogue with the reader and general reflections on the art of fiction. The introductory chapters also range widely but they concentrate on the art of the 'new Province of Writing' of which the author declares he is 'the Founder' (II, i; 77), and the reader's task is to assemble these separate comments into a body of theory, and to collate the theory and practice of the book.

The introductory chapters to Books Two and Four, for example, are concerned to distinguish *Tom Jones* from existing forms of fiction. They define what it is by stating what it is not. It is 'not a Life; nor an Apology for a Life', but may more appropriately be called a 'History' (II, i; 75). On the other hand it avoids the excesses of 'the painful and voluminous Historian' who loses the significance of the events he relates in a sea of detail. In *Tom Jones* events will receive the treatment their significance warrants. The author has absolute power to decide what is and is not significant, but he intends to exercise that power benignly:

> I am, indeed, set over them for their own Good only, and was created for their Use, and not they for mine. Nor do I doubt, while I make their Interest the great Rule of my Writings, they will unanimously concur in supporting my Dignity, and in rendering me all the Honour I shall deserve or desire. (78)

Authors and readers have interlocking rights and duties, from which both benefit in a well-conducted fictional world. This covenant with the reader, and the earlier insistence that everything included will be significant, combine to assure him that if the form is a new one, it is a deliberate and considered one. The tone, half-serious and half-bantering, promises that the new mixture will be entertaining as well as challenging. Most major works of fiction redefine the nature of fiction to some degree, though few parade their originality so forthrightly. In the first chapter of Book Four the author is even more light-hearted. In place of a 'Tankard of good Ale', which would 'refresh the Mind, whenever those Slumbers which in a long Work are apt to invade the Reader as well as the Writer ... begin to creep upon him', he promises: 'sundry Similes,

Descriptions, and other kind of poetical Embellishments' (150–1). As usual, however, he also has a serious point to make, which is to distinguish his work from:

> those idle Romances which are filled with Monsters, the Productions, not of Nature, but of distempered Brains; and which have been therefore recommended by an eminent Critic to the sole Use of the Pastry-cook. (150)

These romances lack the 'Truth' of *Tom Jones*: particularly in their invention of characters who bear little relation to human nature.

In the introductory chapter to Book Three then the reader is encouraged to use 'that wonderful Sagacity, of which he is Master' (116) to predict how the principal characters would behave before the author tells him:

> it is a more useful Capacity to be able to foretel the Actions of Men in any Circumstance from their Characters; than to judge of their Characters from their Actions. The former, I own, requires the greater Penetration; but may be accomplished by true Sagacity, with no less Certainty than the latter. (117)

It would be difficult to find a more succinct description of the characterization in *Tom Jones*. What is said applies both to the fictional world, in which the reader may play at sagacity in a controlled environment, and thereby develop his talents, and to the real world, in which his surviving and prospering may well depend on his ability to judge, and to predict correctly, the actions of others. The book is therefore designed to expose the reader to fictional examples which will exercise and test his judgement of character. There is no point practising on 'idle Romances', since the examples of human nature they offer are too far removed from those encountered in the real world. The comparison emphasizes that to read *Tom Jones* as if it were an escapist fantasy is to misread it. While the plot has similarities to romance, its ending has to be earned, by Tom and by reader, in a replica of the real world, and not in fantasy.

An interesting example which develops throughout the book and which tests the skill of Tom, Allworthy, and the reader is the characterization of Black George Seagrim. Most of this is developed in the first third of the book, but it extends through to Book Eighteen. I intend to consider it in its entirety here because it illustrates how Fielding uses a series of contexts to complicate the judgemental process for his characters and the reader.

While still a boy Tom steadfastly refuses to betray Black George when the pair have been shooting partridges, and Tom has been caught pursuing them into a neighbour's property (III, ii), and there are numerous other instances of Tom helping the Seagrim family. While he is eventually rewarded with Molly's favours, the author is at pains to point out that it is Molly and not Tom who initiates the relationship, though Tom holds himself responsible (IV, vi). When Tom loses the £500 Allworthy gives him on his expulsion from Paradise Hall, Black George finds it, and when he meets the distraught Tom almost immediately he does not return the money, though he does agree to take a farewell letter to Sophia. The author comments:

> I believe there are few Favours which he would not have gladly conferred on Mr. *Jones*; for he bore as much Gratitude towards him as he could, and was as honest as Men who love Money better than any other Thing in the Universe generally are. (VI, xii; 314)

That might well have been the end of the matter, but it is not. Sophia sends Tom her purse containing sixteen guineas via Black George, who considers keeping that money too:

> His Conscience, however, immediately started at this Suggestion, and began to upbraid him with Ingratitude to his Benefactor. To this his Avarice answered, 'That his Conscience should have considered that Matter before, when he deprived poor *Jones* of his 500 *l*. That having quietly acquiesced in what was of so much greater Importance, it was absurd, if not downright Hypocrisy, to affect any Qualms at this Trifle.' In return to which, Conscience, like a good Lawyer, attempted to distinguish between an absolute Breach of Trust, as here where the Goods were delivered, and a bare Concealment of what was found, as in the former Case. Avarice presently treated this with Ridicule, called it a Distinction without a Difference, and absolutely insisted, that when once all Pretensions of Honour and Virtue were given up in any one Instance, that there was no Precedent for resorting to them upon a second Occasion. In short, poor Conscience had certainly been defeated in the Argument, had not Fear stept in to her Assistance, and very strenuously urged, that the real Distinction between the two Actions, did not lie in the different Degrees of Honour, but of Safety: For that the secreting the 500 *l*. was a Matter of very little Hazard; whereas the detaining the Sixteen Guineas was liable to the utmost Danger of Discovery.

> By this friendly Aid of Fear, Conscience obtained a compleat Victory in the Mind of *Black George,* and after making him a few Compliments on his Honesty, forced him to deliver the Money to *Jones.* (VI, xiii; 319–20)

This long comment makes it clear that Black George's motives are more complex than mere greed. The author dramatizes a confrontation of the conflicting motives of conscience, avarice, and fear. The satiric tone is reminiscent of *Joseph Andrews,* where, for example, Mrs Slipslop rationalizes Joseph's refusal of her advances with the aid of philosophy derived from a stone-bottle of liquor (I, ix; 44), and had the scene occurred in the earlier novel, it is unlikely that anything would have been added to so deft an exposition of the triumph of base motives over hypocritically assumed better ones.

But the author of *Tom Jones* is not prepared to let the matter rest there. Instead, the satirical force of the passage is modified, later, in an explicit directive to the reader, advising him not to judge George as the earlier satire seems to direct, but rather to remember that: 'it is often the same Person who represents the Villain and the Heroe; and he who engages your Admiration To-day, will probably attract your Contempt To-Morrow' (VII, i; 327). This further discussion of Black George's behaviour occurs in a key introductory chapter, entitled 'A Comparison between the World and the Stage', in which the author elaborates on some of the major themes of the book, and in which, typically, he starts with a stock comparison, which he reactivates by approaching it in a fresh and novel manner.[11] In all previous comparisons of life and the theatre, he says, 'the Resemblance hath been always taken from the Stage only. None, as I remember, have at all considered the Audience at this great Drama' (325). He proceeds to imagine the varied reactions of a contemporary theatre audience to Black George's ingratitude to 'his Friend and Benefactor'. The upper gallery, which contained footmen, vented 'scurrilous Reproach'; the middle gallery, which contained the lower middle class, was less noisy but no less hostile; the pit, which contained the critics, was divided between the author's friends, who found the scene villainous but natural, and the would-be critics, who 'called it Low, and fell a Groaning'; and finally the boxes, which contained the quality, who were politely inattentive and unwilling to risk an opinion.

---

[11] Sheridan Baker describes Fielding's reworking of clichés in 'Henry Fielding and the Cliché', *Criticism,* Vol. 1, 1959, pp. 354–61.

If it is surprising to find the paltry behaviour of Black George made the subject for so elaborate a reflection, it soon becomes clear that it has been chosen deliberately because it seems beneath consideration. The true judgement of men is a central theme of *Tom Jones*, and Black George is an example of how easy it is to judge too quickly and superficially. Indeed the author had previously almost allowed himself to condemn the man. But when we look at the audience, instead of at the action, we see all too clearly that those who condemn unthinkingly are themselves naturally fallible, and all too open to similar strictures. The author, who is 'admitted behind the Scenes of this great Theatre of Nature', knows that as Garrick, the greatest of tragic actors, 'sometimes condescends to play the Fool', so the wisest men have at times 'played the Fool egregiously in Earnest' (327–8). No man is wise at all hours, and no wise man expects others to be so. Men are given their parts to play by the passions that rise within them, just as actors are given their parts to play in the theatre. Judgement, therefore, should proceed cautiously, since an actor is hardly to be taken to task for the moral worth of the character he portrays, though if he cannot find himself in sympathy with the character his playing will lack authenticity. 'Upon the whole then,' the author concludes, 'the Man of Candour, and of true Understanding, is never hasty to condemn. He can censure an Imperfection, or even a Vice, without Rage against the guilty Party.' The reader of *Tom Jones* is clearly expected to endorse this sentiment, and to dissociate himself from the ready condemnation of most of the theatre audience, unless, that is, he wishes to forfeit the good opinion of the author.

The choice of the stage analogy is an interesting one, which recurs throughout the book, as we shall see. It is here used to present the author's theory of the relationship between art and life, which is a cornerstone of his theory of fiction. The right judging of a stage villain is parallel to, though distinct from, the right judging of a villain in life. The similarities are stressed:

> Some have considered the larger Part of Mankind in the Light of Actors, as personating Characters no more their own, and to which, in Fact, they have no better Title, than the Player hath to be in Earnest thought the King or Emperor whom he represents. Thus the Hypocrite may be said to be a Player; and indeed the *Greeks* called them both by one and the same Name. (324)

But the author has earlier been at pains to distinguish between the judgement of fictional characters and those in life. Commenting upon

Allworthy's employment of Thwackum as tutor to Tom and Blifil, he writes:

> For the Reader is greatly mistaken, if he conceives that *Thwackum* appeared to Mr. *Allworthy* in the same Light as he doth to him in this History; and he is as much deceived, if he imagines, that the most intimate Acquaintance which he himself could have had with that Divine, would have informed him of those Things which we, from our Inspiration, are enabled to open and discover. Of Readers who from such Conceits as these, condemn the Wisdom or Penetration of Mr. *Allworthy*, I shall not scruple to say, that they make a very bad and ungrateful Use of that Knowledge which we have communicated to them. (III, v; 135)

While this is in part a defence of Allworthy's judgement and penetration—two fundamental qualities of the wise man as postulated in *Tom Jones*—it is also a clear distinction between what we can know of characters in the play world of art, and what we can know of other people in life. As E. M. Forster puts it:

> it brings out the fundamental difference between people in daily life and people in books. In daily life we never understand each other . . . But people in a novel can be understood completely by the reader, if the novelist wishes.[12]

The author of *Tom Jones* is acutely aware of the privileges he enjoys in presenting his fictional characters to the reader, a privilege earned by the perception which allows him to be admitted behind the scenes of human nature. The complex fate of the novelist, as he sees it, is to follow nature scrupulously, like a good actor, while at the same time reminding his reader not to mistake the artificial world of fiction for the real world in which he lives. The admonition to the reader regarding Allworthy's judgement of Thwackum is a grim reminder that the privileges of art do not extend to life, that the hypocrisy which may be rendered ineffectual and comic by the omniscience of the artist is anything but comic in ordinary experience.

No doubt a real Tom Jones would not have found Black George's ingratitude easy to forgive, but in the novel the author continues his defence of him even beyond the full discussion we have been examining.

---

[12] *Aspects of the Novel*, Harmondsworth 1962, p. 54.

In a later introductory chapter (XII, i) there is a revealing analogy when in a discussion of literary plagiarism the author claims the same right to pillage the ancient writers that the poor of every parish claim to pillage the squire. In stealing from Tom, George is exercising this immemorial right, though the fact that Tom is not exactly the squire complicates his problem and weakens his rationalization. The author accepts this right—with how much irony it is impossible to say precisely—and even uses it in his own defence. And later again in the novel George helps Tom by smuggling letters to Sophia when she is imprisoned by her father in London, at some risk to his position with Squire Western (XVI, iii; 842). This disinterested act of gratitude contrasts strongly with the earlier theft. Finally, however, Allworthy refuses Tom's plea that George be pardoned. Tom urges the size of the temptation as an ameliorating circumstance:

> Consider, Sir, what a Temptation to a Man who hath tasted such bitter Distress, it must be to have a Sum in his Possession, which must put him and his Family beyond any future Possibility of suffering the like. (XVIII, xi; 969)

Allworthy replies that Tom is too forgiving:

> Such mistaken Mercy is not only Weakness, but borders on Injustice, and is very pernicious to Society, as it encourages Vice. The Dishonesty of this Fellow I might perhaps have pardoned, but never his Ingratitude. (969)

Tom yields to Allworthy's vehemence, though later, when Black George has run away to avoid retribution, he gives the £500 to George's family (XVIII, xiii; 980). The author does not reveal his own ultimate assessment of this conflict between justice and mercy, and the reader is left with a multiple choice. He may condemn the thief, or only the theft. He may excuse, or at least condone it, as ordinary human weakness. Or he may draw the Shavian conclusion that morality is dependent on the size of the temptation. That the author has gone to such lengths to complicate a seemingly simple moral assessment is a measure of how far the comic art of *Tom Jones* rises above Fielding's earlier satire. 'The authorial command of *Tom Jones*', says Claude Rawson, 'has to be earned . . . by a continuous and vital plasticity of relationship between moral urgency and urbane detachment'.[13] Both of these qualities contribute to the final view of Black

---

[13] *Henry Fielding and the Augustan Ideal under Stress*, p. 245.

George and Tom, a view made morally comprehensive by the use of different contexts spaced through the book to explore its different aspects.

In Books Three and Four the three main characters of the younger generation emerge, and the relationships which develop between them as children foreshadow those which will constitute the main action of the book. A kinship grows up between Tom and Sophia when they are children, and when they mature Tom is attracted by Sophia's beauty, by her superior mind and heart, by her reciprocation of his feelings, and by the wisdom that, as her name indicates, she represents. Allworthy tells Tom early in the story (V, vii; 244) that he lacks prudence (the worldly application of wisdom), and he is to spend the book learning first that he needs to acquire it, and finally what it is. To clarify this process Tom is paired with a contrary character. Blifil has in abundance that debased form of prudence which will see him through in a corrupt world. Tom needs prudence to protect him from that same world, and indeed from the plots of Blifil, but the prudence he is to learn is derived from the wisdom of Sophia, and is the generous Christian virtue of prudence, not the self-seeking 'prudence' of the hypocrite. Sophia, alone of the main characters, is not provided with a counterpart, though she is compared with various other characters. Outside the book there is of course Charlotte Fielding, upon whom the author tells us she was modelled (IV, ii; 156). Sophia alone combines good-nature, virtue, and a sure intuitive judgement of character. At an early age she is able to see the truth about Tom and Blifil, a perception which causes her much hardship in the book, but which ensures her eventual happiness. She needs no foil, apart from that provided by the lesser mortals in the book. If she is idealized to some extent she is also humanized. We see her vanity, in dressing her best to see Tom (XVIII, xii; 970); her guile, in putting off her aunt's insistence on the Fellamar marriage with adroit questions about Miss Western's supposed refusal of a coronet (XVII, iv; 890); and her well-founded suspicion that her cousin Mrs Fitzpatrick, though protesting spotless virtue, 'was really not better than she should be' (XI, x; 615–16). She is not presented for the uncritical admiration of the reader but she is the most attractive, intelligent, and perceptive character in the novel, the standard by which human nature at its best is to be measured.

The introduction of such a character into an ironic work like *Tom Jones* requires considerable authorial tact to keep the portrait from lapsing into bathos, that deadliest of Augustan literary sins. Sophia is given a set-piece introduction at the beginning of Book Four, the introductory chapter of which is a mock apology for: 'those ornamental Parts of our

Work . . . where we are about to introduce a considerable Character on the Scene' (152). After some comic and satiric quips about theatrical, political, and royal processions, the author announces that:

> Our Intention, in short, is to introduce our Heroine with the utmost Solemnity in our Power, with an Elevation of Stile, and all other Circumstances proper to raise the Veneration of our Reader. (IV, i; 154)

There is a hint of self-mockery here, as there is in the title of the following chapter: 'A short Hint of what we can do in the Sublime, and a Description of Miss *Sophia Western*', which leaves the reader unsure whether to expect a sublime or a mock-heroic description. What he gets is a dextrous balancing of the two. The heroine is ushered in with a fanfare of classical splendour:

> Do thou, sweet *Zephyrus*, rising from thy fragrant Bed, mount the western Sky, and lead on those delicious Gales, the Charms of which call forth the lovely *Flora* from her Chamber, perfumed with pearly Dews, when on the first of *June*, her Birth-day, the blooming Maid, in loose Attire, gently trips it over the verdant Mead, where every Flower rises to do her Homage, till the whole Field becomes enamelled, and Colours contend with Sweets which shall ravish her most. (154)

After two paragraphs of rapture, which tremble on the edge of self-ridiculing extravagance without ever quite toppling over, the author abruptly changes style, and drops into a chatty colloquy with the reader. With the help of some anecdotes, and scraps of poetry, he enumerates Sophia's physical charms in considerable detail. Her mental accomplishments, however, are passed over briefly, since:

> as there are no Perfections of the Mind which do not discover themselves, in that perfect Intimacy, to which we intend to introduce our Reader, with this charming young Creature; so it is needless to mention them here: Nay, it is a Kind of tacit Affront to our Reader's Understanding, and may also rob him of that Pleasure which he will receive in forming his own Judgment of her Character. (157)

This adroit tossing of the ball back into the reader's court completes the rhetorically impressive introduction of the heroine, in which the author has elevated his style, in accord with the worth of the subject, but in a gently ironic way, which filters off the bathos which threatens such a description, and leaves the unpretentious and charming excellence of Sophia entire. She is thus lifted to a plane above the comic world of the rest of the novel, yet because this is achieved through partly comic description, no violence is done to the pervading tone of the work. The portrait is an achievement of considerable skill and tact on the part of the author, and the reader is invited to observe the art with which it is presented, and to test it both against nature, and those literary imitations of nature quoted or imitated in the passage. That Sophia emerges fresh and natural from all this artifice vindicates the author's method. It is difficult to see how he could have achieved so fine a balance between sublimity and comedy without the self-conscious artificiality with which he goes about the portrait. Sophia emerges as a heroine who is no 'heroine', one who is admired but not romanticized, and one who belongs to the tradition of Shakespeare's and Molière's capable, self-confident, and enterprising young women. As the novel unfolds her character is clarified, as we shall see, within the outlines sketched in this introductory portrait, which displays, succinctly and light-heartedly, as sublime a character as the true limits of human nature allow.

If Sophia is the heroine of the book, Blifil is its villain. As a boy, he is referred to as Master Blifil, and the use of his surname in contrast to the use of Tom's first name suggests that he is already an adult figure while Tom remains engagingly boyish. The characterization of Blifil is not regarded as one of the successes of *Tom Jones*—he lacks the vitality of Jonathan Wild, and the menace of the noble lord in *Amelia*—but comedy is not the place for Iagos and Gonerils. Blifil is a hypocrite, almost a very successful hypocrite, and if he lacks a human dimension it is perhaps because Fielding judges hypocrisy to be the most inhuman of vices. The portrayal of the vice, if not of the man, is skilfully done, drawing forth as it does Fielding's characteristic techniques for exposing the real, ignoble motive behind the pretended, respectable one. When Tom sells his Bible, for example, to help the dismissed Black George support his family, it is bought by Blifil:

> though he had already such another of his own, partly out of Respect for the Book, and partly out of Friendship to *Tom*, being unwilling that the Bible should be sold out of the Family at half Price. He therefore disbursed the said half Price himself; for he was a very prudent Lad, and so careful of his Money, that he had laid up almost every Penny which he had received from Mr. *Allworthy*.
>
> Some People have been noted to be able to read in no Book but their own. On the contrary, from the Time when Master *Blifil* was first possessed of this Bible, he never used any other. Nay, he was seen

reading in it much oftner than he had before been in his own. Now, as he frequently asked *Thwackum* to explain difficult Passages to him, that Gentleman unfortunately took Notice of *Tom's* Name, which was written in many Parts of the Book. This brought on an Enquiry, which obliged Master *Blifil* to discover the whole Matter. (III, ix; 144–5)

If there were no other mention of Blifil in the novel, we might know him from this brief scene, in which he is observed from an authorial point of view which is shared by the reader, but not by the other characters. No one but the author, with his special knowledge, could write from this vantage, and give the reader access to disguised motivation. This access is not, however, handed over flatly. It is dramatized so that the reader progressively discovers for himself the truth behind the appearances of the incident. The author begins by citing respect and friendship, the motives Blifil hypocritically assumes in buying the Bible, and then undermines their validity by allowing the reader to observe Blifil's meanness, his scheming malevolence, his sycophantic manipulation of Thwackum, and the contrast between his 'prudence' and Tom's generous motive for selling the book. Mean though he is, Blifil is willing to spend his money to discredit Tom.

The most surprising thing about Blifil is his success in deceiving Allworthy and Tom. We later discover that Tom was not entirely ignorant of his character. He says to Dowling:

> I own I never greatly liked him. I thought he wanted that Generosity of Spirit, which is the sure Foundation of all that is great and noble in Human Nature. I saw a Selfishness in him long ago which I despised; but it is lately, very lately, that I have found him capable of the basest and blackest Designs; for, indeed, I have at last found out, that he hath taken an Advantage of the Openness of my own Temper, and hath concerted the deepest Project, by a long Train of wicked Artifice, to work my Ruin, which at last he hath effected. (XII, x; 657)

Tom then is not as imperceptive of his sibling's character as he may earlier have seemed, but he was unaware of the plot against himself. Both Tom and Allworthy, and Parson Adams in *Joseph Andrews*, personify Fielding's radical concept of innocence, which leaves the truly good man particularly open to the practices of hypocrisy, because of the entire innocence of such evil in his own nature. Tom and Allworthy are more worldly than Adams, though still limited in their perception of evil by their own lack of it. Sophia, who uniquely combines true goodness with perceptive judgement, is less easy to deceive. Blifil has made an early mistake with her in releasing her pet bird, and Sophia, who has shown a marked preference for Tom over Blifil, imputes his action to anger at being thus slighted (IV, iii; 159). Blifil is able to persuade Allworthy, Square, and Thwackum that the bird languished after liberty, and that he released it on principle. But he fails with Tom, who 'cursed *Blifil* for a pitiful, malicious Rascal' (160), with Western, whose self-interest causes him to ignore protestations of principle (164), and with Sophia, who discerned:

> that *Tom*, though an idle, thoughtless, rattling Rascal, was no-body's Enemy but his own; and that Master *Blifil*, though a prudent, discreet, sober young Gentleman, was at the same Time strongly attached to the Interest only of one single Person. (IV, v; 165)

When Blifil later comes courting Sophia he is consequently at a disadvantage, and is unable to win her confidence. The author chooses not to describe the interview, but he comments that:

> It is possible the great Art used by *Blifil* at this Interview, would have prevailed on *Sophia* to have made another Man in his Circumstances her Confident, and to have revealed the whole Secret of her Heart to him; but she had contracted so ill an Opinion of this young Gentleman, that she was resolved to place no Confidence in him: For Simplicity, when set on its Guard, is often a Match for Cunning. (VII, vi; 344)

Sophia is woman enough to trust her intuitive judgement of Blifil rather than listen to the skilful rhetoric with which he approaches her. And we cannot help wondering whether Bridget, who was a good deal less innocent than Sophia, did not also see her son for what he was, particularly as we are told that she, like Sophia, preferred Tom (III, vi; 139). She had 'absolutely hated' her husband, and she 'certainly hated her own Son' (139), the product of her marriage to Captain Blifil. But we are not told if she saw through his hypocrisy, in particular if she divined his purpose to discredit her favourite Tom. If she did, she was perhaps kept silent by the fear of admitting her lapse with Tom's father, Mr Summer, and by her knowledge that she could always foil any plan to alienate Tom from Allworthy by confessing the truth of his birth.

Blifil's plot against Tom, though maliciously designed and patiently and determinedly pursued, and though it is aided by Bridget's death and Allworthy's innocence, never really becomes tragically threatening. Like the Don John counterplot in *Much Ado About Nothing*, which casts a dark shadow over the fine raillery of Beatrice and Benedick, and the honest passion of Hero and Claudio, but which is foiled by the base instruments it uses, and by the bumbling honesty of Dogberry and Verges, the Blifil plot, while complicating the middle stages of the action, never seems in real danger of succeeding. In both works the vitality, the 'animal spirits' and the essential goodness of the principals so light up the scene that the conspiracy against them is forced to haunt its fringes. The shadowy villains who remain there nonetheless serve to remind us how quickly comedy becomes tragedy when they take on flesh and blood and move to centre stage.

At his first introduction, however, Blifil is by no means dismissed as an opponent of Tom, and his threat to Sophia is presented, not only as thoroughly nasty, but as uncomfortably like the worst passion of a Lovelace, determined to subdue a spirited and attractive girl into a helpless, if hostile, sex object:

> Tho' Mr. *Blifil* was not of the Complexion of *Jones*, nor ready to eat every Woman he saw, yet he was far from being destitute of that Appetite which is said to be the common Property of all Animals. With this, he had likewise that distinguishing Taste, which serves to direct Men in their Choice of the Objects, or Food of their several Appetites; and this taught him to consider *Sophia* as a most delicious Morsel, indeed to regard her with the same Desires which an Ortolan inspires into the Soul of an Epicure. Now the Agonies which affected the Mind of *Sophia* rather augmented than impaired her Beauty; for her Tears added Brightness to her Eyes, and her Breasts rose higher with her Sighs. Indeed no one hath seen Beauty in its highest Lustre, who hath never seen it in Distress. *Blifil* therefore looked on this human Ortolan with greater Desire than when he viewed her last; nor was his Desire at all lessened by the Aversion which he discovered in her to himself. On the contrary, this served rather to heighten the Pleasure he proposed in rifling her Charms, as it added Triumph to Lust; nay, he had some further Views, from obtaining the absolute Possession of her Person, which we detest too much even to mention; and Revenge itself was not without its Share in the Gratifications which he promised himself. The rivalling poor *Jones*, and supplanting him in her Affections, added another Spur to his Pursuit, and promised another additional Rapture to his Enjoyment. (VII, vi; 345–6)

Blifil has none of the rakish glamour which draws Clarissa to Lovelace, and Sophia lacks Clarissa's masochistic attraction to the dominant male, so there is no chance that either will mistake their antagonism for attraction. Blifil's plans are thus destined to remain a fantasy in which he indulges himself by imagining Sophia to be entirely within his power. The reader can only learn of such fantasies from the character himself or from the author, and as Blifil is not given to soliloquy, we learn his thoughts from the author, who presents them with aloof distaste, and with a repeated unwillingness to describe their unpleasant details. There is no sympathy in this passage, as there is, for example, in the depiction of Lady Booby's lust for Joseph Andrews, in which the character is allowed to speak for herself (IV, xiii). The author's speaking for Blifil has a double effect: it directs the reader's response with comments like 'which we detest too much even to mention'; and it exposes Blifil's real thoughts while draining him of independent life. He becomes a character secured within the author's providential control, and one who arouses more contempt than fear. But if he is thus confined in the book, it is clear that the threat he poses would be altogether more menacing in a comparable situation in life. The fictional world in which the author, safe in his heaven, can expose the schemes of the villain, reminds the reader that in his world not even the wisest man can see into other men's hearts, and that he should therefore beware of being deceived by sober lies.

Blifil may be no rake, but Tom comes dangerously close to acting like one at times, being, as the author says, 'ready to eat every Woman he saw' (VII, vi; 345). The contrast between their sexual appetites is part of the larger contrast between hero and villain, and that in turn is an example of the principle of contrast on which the author tells us the entire work is based:

> Contrast . . . runs through all the Works of the Creation, and may probably have a large Share in constituting in us the Idea of all Beauty, as well natural as artificial: For what demonstrates the Beauty and Excellence of any thing, but its Reverse? Thus the Beauty of Day, and that of Summer, is set off by the Horrors of Night and Winter. And I believe, if it was possible for a Man to have seen only the two former, he would have a very imperfect Idea of their Beauty. (V, i; 212)

This passage occurs in an introductory chapter purporting to explain the inclusion of: 'those initial Essays which we have prefixed to the historical Matter contained in every Book' (209), but which goes about that task enigmatically to say the least. The statement of the principle of contrast, for example, is followed by three illustrations which are singularly inappropriate to the art of *Tom Jones*. The first, describing the industriousness of ladies to procure, or even to act as, foils for one another, suggests that if there are beauties in the work, there are also parts of it as unattractive as the ladies of Bath in the mornings, which not even the facetious author of *Tom Jones* would seriously suggest about his work. The second illustration is the English pantomime, an old enemy of Fielding's, both the serious and the comic elements of which are said to be deadly dull:

> for the *Comic* was certainly duller than any thing before shewn on the Stage, and could be set off only by that superlative Degree of Dulness, which composed the *Serious*. (214)

Once again this is hardly applicable to the art of contrast in *Tom Jones*. The third illustration suggests that when Homer nods, or Oldmixon puts his readers to sleep, they are following the principle enunciated by Steele in *The Tatler*, 'who', the author says, 'told the Public, that whenever he was dull, they might be assured there was a Design in it' (215). While this is amusing enough, it serves only to tease the reader looking for the real point of the chapter, and in his last paragraph the author admits that he has obscured not illuminated his meaning:

> In this Light then, or rather in this Darkness, I would have the Reader to consider these initial Essays. And after this Warning, if he shall be of Opinion, that he can find enough of Serious in other Parts of this History, he may pass over these, in which we profess to be laboriously dull, and begin the following Books, at the second Chapter. (215)

The contrast is certainly not between the comic and the serious, since many of the initial chapters, including the one under consideration, are as comic as anything in the narrative, and the narrative includes both elements. The real contrast between the essays and the narrative, which the reader is left to discover for himself, is that between action and reflection. This is not, of course, a complete separation, as the narrative contains much reflection, though this is usually confined to particular effects and directly related to the action. The essays for their part are not concerned solely with the art of fiction, or with criticism in the literary sense. They reveal the critical mind at work, seeking those general principles which relate the writer to the reader, and the art of fiction to the art of life. Fielding, like Marvell, believed men should 'both act and know'.[14]

The particular contrast between Tom and Blifil is one of many pairings in the narrative which further illustrate the principle expounded in this

---

[14] 'An Horatian Ode', Hugh MacDonald (ed.), *The Poems of Andrew Marvell*, London 1956, p. 120.

chapter. In setting Tom's sexual enthusiasm against Blifil's apparent temperance the author might appear to be reversing received morality. While this should alert the reader to proceed with caution it has not always been effective. Tom's lapses have been attacked as immoral and defended as realistic but they have not always been examined as carefully as they deserve. In each of the three parts of the book depicting country, road, and city, Tom has a sexual adventure which is juxtaposed with his continuing love for Sophia. In the first six-book unit, set in the country, Tom encounters the appropriately bucolic Molly Seagrim, who, as we have seen, seduces him while convincing him, because he is innocent and 'she behaved at last with all decent Reluctance' (IV, vi; 175), that he has seduced her. This happens before Tom is aware of Sophia as a possible partner, though his relations with Molly are not ended by his falling in love with Sophia. Tom's first response to Molly's generosity with her favours is a characteristically generous and unselfish one, which is judiciously endorsed by the author:

> our Heroe ... considered this poor Girl as one whose Happiness or Misery he had caused to be dependent on himself. Her Beauty was still the Object of Desire, though greater Beauty, or a fresher Object, might have been more so; but the little Abatement which Fruition had occasioned to this, was highly over-balanced by the Considerations of the Affection which she visibly bore him, and of the Situation into which he had brought her. The former of these created Gratitude, the latter Compassion; and both together with his Desire for her Person, raised in him a Passion, which might, without any great Violence to the Word, be called *Love*; though, perhaps, it was at first not very judiciously placed. (IV, vi; 175–6)

Tom then is humanly mistaken about the object of his affections, but his affections themselves are attractive and indeed admirable. He is disabused about Molly's dependence on him in one of the gloriously funny incidents which illuminate *Tom Jones*, the discovery behind Molly's rug of the Philosopher Square: 'among other female Utensils ... in a Posture ... as ridiculous as can possibly be conceived' (V, v; 229). Molly had just been protesting that she would always hate and despise the whole male sex for Tom's sake when the rug falls and exposes, among other things, her hypocrisy. Her sister Betty completes the exposure by telling Tom that Will Barnes, not he, had first seduced Molly and fathered her child. Tom's response is to rib Square a little for his pompous hypocrisy, but to keep his secret, and to feel 'perfectly easy ... with Regard to *Molly*' (V, vi; 235).

But when Molly loses her claim to Tom's heart, '*Sophia* took absolute Possession of it' (235). He learns that his feelings are reciprocated, and his crisis of conscience about how to proceed begins. It is interrupted by Allworthy's sickness. When Allworthy recovers, Tom, drunk with wine and joy, is about to carve Sophia's name on every tree when Molly appears, and they soon retire 'into the thickest Part of the Grove' (V, x; 257). That Tom, inspired with love for Sophia, should so readily be inflamed with desire for Molly, fresh from work and none too clean, requires some comment, and the author obliges with a long paragraph reflecting on Tom's behaviour. The paragraph is a defence of Tom only in the legal sense that it says all that an able counsel might say if he were on trial, as indeed he is, before the reader. The author adopts the role of defence attorney, leaving judgement to the reader. This enables him to plead eloquently for Tom without necessarily approving of what he has done. The tone is also legal, with much citing of authorities and precedents, and with an overtone of playfulness not out of place between counsel and judge, for whom the law is something of a game and the opposing parties changing minor figures. The substance of the defence is that Tom was drunk, and while this may not be a strictly legal defence, it is a very human one in sexual matters.[15]

By itself this defence is less than compelling, but it is supported by the careful framing of the incident. Even the author's plea serves a narrative function. The parley between Molly and the wine-laden Tom is too intimate to be described, and in such cases some diversion is necessary. The plea also allows some time to elapse, so that when Blifil and Thwackum appear on the scene, Tom will be caught *in flagrante delicto*. He then defends Molly from discovery by fighting with Thwackum and Blifil while she makes her escape. The battle, like others in the book, is introduced with a fine rhetorical flourish, and with an appropriate blend of classical and animal imagery. Tom wins it, with the help of Western, who arrives on the scene with Sophia. Sophia faints at the sight of Tom covered in blood, and Tom revives her with water from a nearby stream. Tom's courage is evident in his defence of Molly against superior odds, and his gallantry in his care for Sophia.

In the incidents which precede the encounter with Molly, Tom appears in an even more favourable light. When Allworthy seems close to death, there is the unlovely spectacle of the members of his household greedily anticipating their inheritances, and discontentedly complaining that they

---

[15] For an excellent discussion of this scene see Miller, *Henry Fielding's 'Tom Jones' and the Romance Tradition*, p. 96.

are less than they merited (V, viii). Blifil receives the message from lawyer Dowling that his mother has died, and, as we later discover, the truth about Tom's parentage, which he conceals for his own benefit against the express wish of his mother. He then insists, against all medical advice, but with the support of Square and Thwackum, that the supposedly dying Allworthy should be immediately informed of his sister's death, in the obvious hope that the news will worsen his condition, and so hasten Blifil's inheritance of the estate. But Allworthy recovers, and the plan goes astray. In his disappointment, Blifil turns nasty. He rebukes Tom for his joy at Allworthy's recovery, when Bridget's death has just been announced, and he insults Tom for not knowing who his parents were, an insult that Tom very properly resents. Throughout this sequence of greed, ingratitude, deception, malice, and hypocrisy, Tom alone behaves well, so much so that the author devotes a separate chapter to describing his concern for his benefactor, to distinguish it more sharply from the behaviour of the other characters. Tom is genuinely grieved at Allworthy's illness and he is overcome with gratitude at his intended generosity to him. He would have prevented the news of Bridget's death reaching Allworthy if he could, and he sits with him while he sleeps, and silences the snoring nurse so that he will not be disturbed. When Allworthy recovers he is elated. Tom emerges from this contrast as the spiritual heir of Allworthy, as well as his natural heir, as later appears. If he immediately falls into the arms of the willing Molly, there will be few readers not predisposed to judge him leniently in the circumstances.

The author, as we have seen, avoids direct judgement of Tom's succumbing to Molly, and suggests that no simple and unambiguous moral assessment is possible. His reticence, and his insistence that the reader must finally judge the issue, can be clarified by comparing the treatment of the incident in the book, and in Tony Richardson's film. In the novel the author begins his comment:

> Some of my Readers may be inclined to think this Event unnatural. However, the Fact is true; and, perhaps, may be sufficiently accounted for, by suggesting that *Jones* probably thought one Woman better than none, and *Molly* as probably imagined two Men to be better than one. (257)

Then follows the case for the defence with its ambiguous discussion about whether Tom's drunkenness mitigates, or as Aristotle and Pittacus would have it, increases his guilt. The film is simpler and cruder. The commentator says:

> To those who find our hero's behaviour startling, the answer is simple. Tom had always thought that any woman was better than none. While Molly never felt that one man was quite as good as two.[16]

The joke has been retained, but the changes in wording make it coarser, and there is no further discussion of the morality of Tom's action. The film's commentator states the thoughts of Tom and Molly omnisciently, where the novel's author is more circumspect, hedging his tentative suggestions with 'some', 'perhaps', and 'probably'. The author balances the judgement of a 'Court of Justice' against that of a 'Court of Conscience', putting the issue before the reader as a complex one. There is no such uncertainty in the film, in which the morality of Tom and Molly's behaviour is never questioned. In many ways the film was remarkably faithful to the spirit of the book, particularly in the self-conscious artifice with which it was presented. It was as much a meta-film, exposing the artifice and illusion used in making a film, as the novel is a meta-novel, revealing the art and artifice of narrative illusion. But the commentary, though retained in the film, was severely truncated, and this resulted in a drastic foreshortening of the moral perspective of the book, with the loss of that tolerant, thoughtful, and balanced assessment that lies at the heart of Fielding's comic vision.

In the introductory chapter to Book Six, 'Of Love', which follows the incidents we have been discussing, the author expounds his ideas on the nature of love, and on the relation between love and desire. He begins by supporting the opinion of the latitudinarian divines against the attacks of those philosophers who deny the existence of disinterested love, and who argue, with Hobbes and Mandeville, that self-interest rules all human behaviour.[17] It is, he argues, their impoverished minds, not human nature, that cannot conceive of 'a kind and benevolent Disposition, which is gratified by contributing to the Happiness of others' (VI, i; 270), and which consequently deny its existence. Love, so defined, is to be distinguished from 'what is commonly called Love, namely, the Desire of satisfying a voracious Appetite with a certain Quantity of delicate white human Flesh' (270), which should more properly be called hunger or desire. 'Esteem and Gratitude are the proper Motives to Love, as Youth

---

[16] Osborne, *Tom Jones: A Film Script*, p. 50.
[17] The fullest account of Fielding's debt to the latitudinarian divines is Martin C. Battestin, *The Moral Basis of Fielding's Art: A Study of Joseph Andrews*, Middletown, Connecticut 1959. There is an excellent discussion of the chapter 'Of Love' in Martin Price, *To the Palace of Wisdom*, New York 1965, pp. 292–3.

and Beauty are to Desire' (270), and the two passions, though by no means always united, can, when they are united, greatly augment one another:

> Love when it operates towards one of a different Sex, is very apt, towards its complete Gratification, to call in the Aid of that Hunger which I have mentioned above; and which it is so far from abating, that it heightens all its Delights to a Degree scarce imaginable by those who have never been susceptible of any other Emotions, than have proceeded from Appetite alone. (270)

The centrality of these reflections to the ideology of *Tom Jones* is apparent in the address to the reader with which the chapter concludes. It is one of the most direct and explicit in the book, and for once there is no bantering tone, no ironic hedging, no speaking the truth with a smiling countenance, to soften its force:

> Examine your Heart, my good Reader, and resolve whether you do believe these Matters with me. If you do, you may now proceed to their Exemplification in the following Pages; if you do not, you have, I assure you, already read more than you have understood; and it would be wiser to pursue your Business, or your Pleasures (such as they are) than to throw away any more of your Time in reading what you can neither taste nor comprehend. (271)

In practice, however, it is not always easy to distinguish love and desire. The author himself recognizes this in his description of Tom's feelings for Molly, already quoted, in which gratitude and compassion combine with desire to raise 'a Passion, which might, without any great Violence to the Word, be called *Love*' (IV, vi; 176). What is missing here is esteem, and what esteem there was for Molly is much diminished by Tom's later discovery of her deception of him.

If the chapter 'Of Love' is unequivocal in its assertion that love is real, and that it includes but transcends desire, the rest of the book makes it clear that distinctions that are easily made in theory, are sometimes hard-won in practice, where mistakes are not uncommon, particularly when the parties are young and inexperienced. And when love is unattainable, as it is for Tom and Sophia for most of the book, desire does not cease, and the satisfaction of it with a willing partner, and where no injury is inflicted, is not the most heinous of human failings. Indeed it is clear that the author prefers the sexual enthusiasm of Tom, albeit sometimes misdirected, to the continence of Blifil, whose 'Appetites were, by Nature, so moderate, that he was able by Philosophy or by Study, or by some other Method, easily to subdue them' (VI, iv; 284).¹⁸ A generous flow of animal spirits tends, in Fielding, to accompany a generous heart, one open to love, and also to responding sympathetically to the needs and feelings of others. In *Joseph Andrews* a chapter is devoted to 'The History of *Betty* the Chambermaid' whose 'Good-nature, Generosity and Compassion' were unfortunately accompanied by such 'warm Ingredients' that she occasionally succumbed to the temptations occasioned by her employment as chambermaid at the Tow-wouses' inn (I, xviii). Apart from listing Betty's virtues, the author is carefully noncommittal in describing her few lapses and her unsuccessful attempt to seduce the handsome Joseph, though it is clear from the tone that he shares Mr Tow-wouse's preference for Betty over his wife, as mean and self-seeking a landlady as any to be found in that none too generous profession. Blifil, like Mrs Tow-wouse, is mean in his desires as well as his affairs. Fielding does not, on the other hand, simply equate sexual warmth with a generous spirit, though he often depicts them in the same people. He is reluctant to condemn characters who are warm in heart and spirit for occasional excesses of sexual warmth, but it is worth stressing that there is no moral vagueness in this, and no easy sentimentality. Betty's first lover, an Ensign of Foot, raised 'a Flame in her, which required the Care of a Surgeon to cool' (86), and Tom is made to suffer for what are clearly seen to be wrong, if human, indulgences. The characters Fielding presents as essentially admirable all err at times, in judgement or behaviour. Having the vices of their virtues, they are open to persuasion as they are openhearted, and they are too easily manipulated by their moral inferiors. Real moral discrimination is required, not only to separate Tom's faults from his virtues, but also to recognize that lapses do not make a good man bad any more than hypocritically assumed virtues make a bad man good. Fielding's characters are mixed, but they are not confused.

As the chapter 'Of Love' indicates, Tom's world is largely populated by those for whom love is an appetite, wisdom the quintessence of self-interest, and prudence 'the art of thriving'.¹⁹ Such people do not negate the existence of love, wisdom, and prudence, but they obscure them by their misuse of the words, and they prey on those who exemplify the real virtues with a ruthlessness vitiated only by their inherent meanness, and the providential intervention of the author. At the time of Allworthy's

---

¹⁸ Robert Alter discusses Fielding's style here in *Fielding and the Nature of the Novel*, p. 44.
¹⁹ See Jack D. Durant, 'The "Art of Thriving" in Fielding's Comedies' in Donald Kay (ed.), *A Provision of Human Nature*, University of Alabama 1977, pp. 25–35.

illness, Tom is treated to a comprehensive demonstration of the corruption of his world. It is no wonder he celebrates when the only good man he knows recovers. And if the celebration results in Tom boarding Molly, and thumping Blifil and Thwackum, it is no more than they ask for, and it demonstrates dramatically the difficulties Tom encounters in learning to live in a corrupt world without becoming tainted himself. Before encountering Molly Tom was worshipping Sophia, and her later arrival with her father enables the scene to end with Tom reaffirming his allegiance to the love, wisdom and prudence which she personifies.

Sophia is the only person besides Allworthy who illuminates the world in which Tom lives. From the time of the incident of the pet bird, her partiality for Tom is clear, and it develops as they grow older. Tom's feelings are muddied by his involvement with Molly, and Sophia's develop almost without her realizing what is happening, but it is plain to the reader that the two are falling in love, and that this is the positive plot which counters the increasing efforts to discredit and to dismiss Tom. The morning after the churchyard battle between Molly and Goody Brown (IV, viii), Tom hunts with Mr Western, and returns with him to dinner:

> The lovely *Sophia* shone forth that Day with more Gaiety and Sprightliness than usual. Her Battery was certainly levelled at our Heroe; though, I believe, she herself scarce yet knew her own Intention; but if she had any Design of charming him, she now succeeded. (IV, x; 187)

Unfortunately, however, Parson Supple relates the story of Molly's battle, and her subsequent appearance before Allworthy, who commits her to Bridewell. At this point Tom leaves abruptly, to plead for Molly, and the hapless Sophia is treated to her father's coarse celebration of Tom's presumed responsibility for Molly's bastard. The incident opens Sophia's eyes to the nature of the feelings she has harboured for Tom, and precipitates a conflict between those feelings and Tom's apparent engagement elsewhere:

> The Situation of this young Lady was now very different from what it had ever been before. That Passion, which had formerly been so exquisitely delicious, became now a Scorpion in her Bosom. (IV, xii; 199)

She resolves to take the practical step of visiting her aunt in order to forget Tom, but is prevented from executing this commendable intention by the hunting accident, in which Tom saves her from a fall, while breaking his arm in the process. When he is confined to Western's house for his convalescence, the courtship proper between Tom and Sophia begins. It is an idyllic interlude in which, for a brief moment, they are 'playmates in an Arcadian world',[20] but reflection on the impossibility of marriage soon disturbs their joy. Tom, like Sophia before him, is surprised and disturbed when he realizes the depth of the feelings that have grown up between them:

> When these Thoughts had fully taken Possession of *Jones*, they occasioned a Perturbation in his Mind, which, in a Constitution less pure and firm than his, might have been, at such a Season, attended with very dangerous Consequences. He was truly sensible of the great Worth of *Sophia*. He extremely liked her Person, no less admired her Accomplishments, and tenderly loved her Goodness. In Reality, as he had never once entertained any Thought of possessing her, nor had ever given the least voluntary Indulgence to his Inclinations, he had a much stronger Passion for her than he himself was acquainted with. His Heart now brought forth the full Secret, at the same Time that it assured him the adorable Object returned his Affection. (V, ii; 220)

The ensuing conflict in Tom is due partly to his recognition that Squire Western would never allow them to marry, and partly to his continuing commitment to Molly. This latter is removed by the discovery of Square behind Molly's rug, and Tom's realization that he is not the father of her child, or her seducer, and not even the primary object of her affections. But the former part of Tom's conflict remains:

> His Heart was now, if I may use the Metaphor, entirely evacuated, and *Sophia* took absolute Possession of it. He loved her with an unbounded Passion, and plainly saw the tender Sentiments she had for him; yet could not this Assurance lessen his Despair of obtaining the Consent of her Father, nor the Horrors which attended his Pursuit of her by any base or treacherous Method. (V, vi; 235)

There seems to be no way in which the lovers can be united, but the reader is less despairing than Tom, and confidently expects that so eminently compatible a hero and heroine will not end up apart. Comedies end in marriage, and *Tom Jones* is already clearly a comedy, for all the menacing shadows which surround its few good people. Despite the emotional conflicts of Tom and Sophia, then, their courtship is a charming study of

[20] Miller, *Henry Fielding's 'Tom Jones' and the Romance Tradition*, p. 67.

dawning regard deepening into love. It culminates in their meeting in the garden immediately before Tom is summoned home to attend Mr Allworthy's illness (V, vi), and though their speech is alternately broken and formal, their communication is eloquent, and their understanding mutual. From this point on the book is concerned with the forces which will separate them before ultimately bringing them together.

To this point Tom's history has, thanks to his mother's scheming, and Allworthy's benevolence, been fortunate, if rather precariously so, and his discovery of Sophia points the direction in which he is to proceed. But as his fortunes rise, so the forces opposing them gather strength. The hypocrites who surround Tom are dedicated to his downfall by their very nature. As Fielding says in his 'An Essay on the Knowledge of the Characters of Men':

> in destroying the Reputation of a virtuous and good Man, the Hypocrite imagines he hath disarmed his Enemy of all Weapons to hurt him; and therefore this sanctified Hypocrisy is not more industrious to conceal its own Vices, than to obscure and contaminate the Virtues of others. As the Business of such a Man's Life is to procure Praise, by acquiring and maintaining an undeserved Character; so is his utmost Care employed to deprive those who have an honest Claim to the Character himself affects only, of all the Emoluments which could otherwise arise to them from it.[21]

The essay attempts to warn the unsuspecting good against the inevitable malice of the envious, a situation that Fielding dramatizes in Tom's expulsion from Paradise Hall in Book Six, and indeed throughout *Tom Jones*. In the introductory chapter to Book Eleven, the author expresses his detestation of slander:

> Vice hath not, I believe, a more abject Slave; Society produces not a more odious Vermin; nor can the Devil receive a Guest more worthy of him, nor possibly more welcome to him, than a Slanderer. (XI, i; 567)

The ostensible subject is the slander of books by critics, but it is extended to include the slander of the men who write them:

> The Slander of a Book is, in Truth, the Slander of the Author: For as no one can call another Bastard, without calling the Mother a Whore,

---

[21] *Miscellanies*, p. 170.

so neither can any one give the Names of sad Stuff, horrid Nonsense, &c. to a Book, without calling the Author a Blockhead; which tho' in a moral Sense it is a preferable Appellation to that of a Villain, is perhaps rather more injurious to his worldly Interest. (569)

The innocently naive like Tom are all too prone to neglect their worldly interest, and this makes them easier prey for the malice they unwittingly arouse in the envious minds which surround them.

Blifil's chief lieutenants in the slandering of Tom are the boy's two tutors, Thwackum and Square, who are introduced to the reader as a pair of caricatured opposites:

> This Gentleman and Mr. *Thwackum* scarce ever met without a Disputation; for their Tenets were, indeed, diametrically opposite to each other. *Square* held human Nature to be the Perfection of all Virtue, and that Vice was a Deviation from our Nature in the same Manner as Deformity of Body is. *Thwackum*, on the contrary, maintained that the human Mind, since the Fall, was nothing but a Sink of Iniquity, till purified and redeemed by Grace. (III, iii; 126)

The opposition is continued in the description of their definitions of 'the amiable Quality of Mercy':

> The two Gentlemen did indeed somewhat differ in Opinion concerning the Objects of this sublime Virtue; by which *Thwackum* would probably have destroyed one half of Mankind, and *Square* the other half. (III, x; 147)

The author defends himself against the charge of caricaturing religion and virtue in the persons of Thwackum and Square:

> it is not Religion or Virtue, but the Want of them which is here exposed. Had not *Thwackum* too much neglected Virtue, and *Square* Religion, in the Composition of their several Systems; and had not both utterly discarded all natural Goodness of Heart, they had never been represented as the Objects of Derision in this History. (III, iv; 129)

The pairing, however, remains artificial, one of those felicitous arrangements on which the comedy of *Tom Jones* is built. The author laughs at the emptiness of the tutors' pedagogic theories, and Tom spends much of his boyhood ignoring their admonitions, which perhaps accounts for their malevolence towards him. Tom's 'natural Goodness of Heart' is both inherent in him, and fostered by his association with Allworthy. It is, however, a rare and essentially unexplained quality in Fielding's fictional world, and one which certainly cannot be learned from tutors like Square and Thwackum, who neither possess nor understand it.

Fielding's attitudes to the efficacy of moral education range from the sceptical to the sanguine. In the 'Essay on the Knowledge of the Characters of Men', he speaks of:

> that very early and strong Inclination to Good or Evil, which distinguishes different Dispositions in Children, in their first Infancy . . . so manifest and extreme a Difference of Inclination or Character, that almost obliges us, I think, to acknowledge some unacquired, original Distinction, in the Nature or Soul of one Man, from that of another.[22]

He did not ever overcome the uncertainty of that 'almost'. Tom and Blifil, who share the same mother, and whose nurture is as close to identical as the sons of different fathers could be, are as opposite morally as Square and Thwackum are philosophically, but nature is not entirely to blame. If it were, Tom and the reader would have nothing to learn in the course of the book, and if Fielding believed that, he would not have written it. Andrew Wright describes the negative side of Fielding's view:

> when, in the very title of Book III, Fielding has announced education to be his subject, he is referring to the bad education offered by two ill-equipped tutors to two ineducable boys.[23]

But there is also a positive side to Fielding's thought. The discussion between Adams and Joseph in *Joseph Andrews* on the merits of various forms of education is a classic example of Fielding's ambivalence. Joseph puts the nature argument:

> I remember when I was in the Stable, if a young Horse was vicious in his Nature, no Correction would make him otherwise; I take it to be equally the same among Men. (III, v; 231)

---

[22] Ibid., p. 154.
[23] *Henry Fielding: Mask and Feast*, London 1965, p. 77. On Fielding's ideas on education see Miller, *Essays on Fielding's Miscellanies*, pp. 215–20; and George Sherburn, 'Fielding's Social Outlook', *Philological Quarterly*, Vol. XXXV, 1956, pp. 1–23.

But this Swiftian analogy is contradicted by Adams's insistence on his own skill as a teacher, and his preference for private over public school education. Fielding, who went to Eton without being corrupted, laughs a little at the parson's prejudices, but the book makes it clear that Adams has taught Joseph, and his other parishioners, well. Though he may not have been able to make the vicious virtuous, he has reinforced virtue in those who have it by the strongest of methods, example, and he has rebuked vice and partly subdued it. When, at the end of *Tom Jones*, Adams is engaged as tutor to the children of Tom and Sophia, there is no suggestion that he will be wasting his time, or simply teaching them how to read Aeschylus. In *Amelia*, Fielding seems convinced that morality can be instilled by a virtuous parent. He says of his heroine:

> This admirable woman never let a day pass without instructing her children in some lesson of religion and morality . . . In which she had such success, that not the least marks of pride, envy, malice, or spite discovered itself in any of their little words or deeds. (IV, iii)[24]

This sounds both fulsome and unlikely—one wonders how she would have coped with Blifil—but it makes the point that Fielding could mock the pretensions of educators, and find an unexplained difference of moral quality in different people, without abandoning education and moral influence as pointless undertakings. He remarks elsewhere in 'An Essay on the Knowledge of the Characters of Men':

> Nothing can be plainer, or more known, than the general Rules of Morality, and yet thousands of Men are thought well employed in reviving our Remembrance, and enforcing our Practice of them.[25]

There is no reason to think that Fielding differed from the general opinion he describes here. If he satirized incompetent and unchristian members of the clergy throughout his work, he also warmly endorsed the genuinely Christian ministry of Adams.

In *Tom Jones* the real lessons that Thwackum and Square have to offer their charges are extra-curricular. They help Blifil to deceive Allworthy and to defame Tom, by lending timely and decisive support to his schemes. They teach Tom, belatedly and by default, that those engaged to instruct the young will all too often betray that trust to their own

[24] Henley, Vol. VI, p. 191.
[25] *Miscellanies*, p. 156.

interest. And they demonstrate to Allworthy and the reader that those who most profess virtue are likely to be found crouching behind Molly Seagrim's rug. If these lessons are not always edifying, they are worth mastering in self-defence, and if Tom had been as tractable a pupil of his worldly interest as Blifil, he might have discovered that his tutors had useful qualifications, though they prudently hid them under a bushel. How little Tom's worldly education has in fact progressed may be gauged from his behaviour in the sequence of events which leads to his expulsion by Allworthy. He has, for example, made Square his enemy without realizing it:

> *Tom Jones* shewed no more Regard to the learned Discourses which this Gentleman would sometimes throw away upon him, than to those of *Thwackum*. He once ventured to make a Jest of the Rule of Right; and at another Time said, He believed there was no Rule in the World capable of making such a Man as his Father (for so Mr. *Allworthy* suffered himself to be called.) (III, v; 134)

Square also favours Blifil over Tom in the hope of pleasing Bridget, with whom the author hints he may have had some success (III, vi; 138), until Tom, on growing up, seemed to become his rival: 'on which Account the Philosopher conceived the most implacable Hatred for our poor Heroe' (III, vi; 140). Then there is the rivalry over Molly, and Tom's generous failure to make public his discovery of Square's hypocrisy, for which the philosopher does not readily forgive him. Indeed he intervenes at a crucial point in Tom's fortunes to poison Allworthy's mind against Tom. When Tom saves Molly from Bridewell by confessing his association with her to Allworthy, Square takes the opportunity to misrepresent Tom's previous support for the Seagrim family, support which he knows has favourably impressed Allworthy as an instance of the generosity he practises himself:

> *Square* therefore embraced this Opportunity of injuring *Jones* in the tenderest Part, by giving a very bad Turn to all these before-mentioned Occurrences. 'I am sorry, Sir,' said he, 'to own I have been deceived as well as yourself. I could not, I confess, help being pleased with what I ascribed to the Motive of Friendship, though it was carried to an Excess, and all Excess is faulty, and vicious; but in this I made Allowance for Youth. Little did I suspect that the Sacrifice of Truth, which we both imagined to have been made to Friendship, was, in reality, a Prostitution of it to a depraved and debauched Appetite . . . He supported the Father in order to corrupt the Daughter'. (IV, xi; 195)

These insinuations are plausible enough to affect Allworthy: 'they certainly stamped in the Mind of *Allworthy* the first bad Impression concerning *Jones*' (196). Tom is left entirely unaware of the malice of Square, which is so dextrously designed and executed that it not only influences Allworthy in the wrong direction, but remains an unspoken, and therefore an undefended charge against Tom. Thwackum tyrannizes over Tom throughout his boyhood from no better motives. He also hopes to please the widow by favouring her son Blifil, and he needs a vent for his half-restrained brutality. If he is less devious than Square, he is just as remorseless in his persecution of Tom.

Blifil, who has learned from Thwackum to garb malice in sanctimoniousness, and from Square to claim plausibly virtuous motives for his vicious behaviour, finally discredits Tom with Allworthy. He has been spurred on by the communication from his mother, intercepted at the time of Allworthy's illness, which reveals Tom's parentage, and consequent precedence over Blifil as Allworthy's heir. This gives Blifil a strong and urgent motive to remove Tom before anyone other than himself and Lawyer Dowling learn the truth. Miss Western's discovery that Sophia and Tom are in love, and Western's violent protests to Allworthy, provide Blifil with the occasion he wants. Discussing the mismatch with Allworthy, he lets slip a baited comment, which Allworthy swallows:

> I know him to be one of the worst Men in the World: For had my dear Uncle known what I have hitherto endeavoured to conceal, he must have long since abandoned so profligate a Wretch. (VI, x; 307)

Blifil, feigning reluctance, then tells Allworthy a grossly distorted version of Tom's behaviour during Allworthy's illness. His story is corroborated by Thwackum, who presumably wants revenge for the beating he had from Tom on that occasion. To the reader, who knows the truth, Allworthy may seem to be easily practised upon, but as the author's warning, already quoted, indicates, the reader's surprise should be directed at the Machiavellian skill with which Blifil deceives Allworthy, and not at Allworthy's credulousness. When charged, as he is, as fairly as the deceptions which have been practised allow, Tom is unable to make an adequate defence:

> Many Disadvantages attended poor *Jones* in making his Defence; nay, indeed he hardly knew his Accusation: For as Mr. *Allworthy*, in recounting the Drunkenness, &c. while he lay ill, out of Modesty sunk every thing that related particularly to himself, which indeed prin-

cipally constituted the Crime, *Jones* could not deny the Charge. His Heart was, besides, almost broken already, and his Spirits were so sunk, that he could say nothing for himself. (VI, xi; 310)

In the circumstances Allworthy judges Tom by what appear to have been his actions. The moral is not simply that Allworthy should have been less easy to deceive, though his example is a cautionary tale directed to the reader, but that in a world peopled largely by hypocrites, the best of men may be led astray by their own soundly-based principles of judgement.

As in the incident of Sophia's pet bird, Allworthy is wrong partly because his very virtue inhibits his perception of vice in others. Tom is also limited by not fully recognizing the nature of his sibling despite such evidence as Blifil's betrayal of confidence in revealing that Black George was with Tom when he pursued the partridge. This revelation costs the gamekeeper his position with Allworthy, a position Tom had suffered much pain to preserve (III, x; 148). The price Tom pays for failing to draw the correct conclusions from Blifil's boyish betrayals is his eventual expulsion from Paradise Hall and his separation from Allworthy and Sophia. He is obliged to learn the hard way the lesson that Fielding's good men have to learn—that virtue is not enough in a wicked world. As the author remarks later in the book:

> There are a Set of Religious, or rather Moral Writers, who teach that Virtue is the certain Road to Happiness, and Vice to Misery in this World. A very wholsome and comfortable Doctrine, and to which we have but one Objection, namely, That it is not true. (XV, i, 709)

Tom and Allworthy need to acquire a self-defensive prudence to protect their virtue from being manipulated by those who recognize it without sharing it. As in a number of other instances we have looked at, Fielding seems to have been in two minds about whether a good man could defend himself adequately against an evil that, by definition, he cannot understand. Heartfree in *Jonathan Wild* is helpless in the face of evil, even when that evil is seen to be incompetent and self-defeating. Adams and Joseph, though more muscularly effective in their own and Fanny's defence, are in no sense men of the world. Amelia does not suspect the men who befriend her husband or her children with the intention of seducing her. It might be argued from this evidence that Fielding believed true virtue was so out of place in the world, that it could never really be reconciled to it. The best it could hope for was the providential protection of God, or of the author in fiction, or of a rare like-minded patron like

Allworthy. Allworthy does manage to do something like justice despite the mistakes forced upon him by a corrupt world in unholy alliance with his own innocence. While giving support to this interpretation, *Tom Jones* also offers contrary evidence, suggesting that the rewards for virtue need not be entirely those of the 'paradise within', or of another, better world beyond the present. Allworthy, however fallible, does ultimately recognize, and reward Tom's virtue. If he is credulous, he is also generous and benevolent, and as he is a man of wealth and power he has the opportunity to practise those virtues extensively. Shortly before his most egregious blunder, the dismissal of Tom, the author introduces 'a Digression concerning true Wisdom, of which Mr. *Allworthy* was in Reality as great a Pattern as he was of Goodness', in which he argues that 'the wisest Man is the likeliest to possess all worldly Blessings in an eminent Degree' (VI, iii; 282), which flatly contradicts the previously quoted introduction to Book Fifteen. There is, of course, some truth in both positions, and Fielding's vision in *Tom Jones* is large enough to embrace both.

The real exemplar of human wisdom in the book is not Allworthy, however, but Sophia, and it is her portrayal in particular which separates *Tom Jones* from Fielding's other works. Sophia is the character who most fully shares that combination of virtue with the clear-sighted perception of evil which is attributed to the author and the reader of Fielding's fiction. As such she represents a crucial bridge between the fictional world, where providential rescue of the good is imperative, and the world of the author and the reader, in which it is possible to be entirely unillusioned about evil without partaking of that evil in one's nature. Sophia is no model of perfection, a type of characterization the author specifically avoids (X, i; 526). She is presented as a thoroughly credible, provincial young girl, who mistakes her own feelings and misjudges her lover, and whose aunt can advise her to learn: 'a little Hypocrisy, which would instruct you how to hide your Thoughts a little better' (VI, v; 287). At the same time she is the only character in the book whose judgement of people is essentially correct, who has the natural penetration to see them for what they are. In a book which defines human wisdom as the just assessment of the behaviour and characters of others, she is thus the pattern of that wisdom. She represents an act of faith in the possibility of combining virtue and penetration, nature and art, both inside and outside the fictional world. The author, who anticipates that 'many of our Readers will probably be in Love' with his heroine (III, x; 149), also assures those readers, as we have seen, that:

many of our fair Country-women will be found worthy to satisfy any Passion, and to answer any Idea of Female Perfection, which our Pencil will be able to raise. (IV, i; 154)

In other words she belongs, and is to be found, in the same world as the reader, who may find his own version of Sophia or Charlotte Fielding. The philosophical consequence is that the self-interest, malice, and hypocrisy which cast so dark a shadow over most of Fielding's work are countered in *Tom Jones* by a central trio of characters who are ultimately able to frustrate their designs, and to demonstrate that virtue may achieve happiness, both personal and material, in a corrupt world.

But it is a near thing, and at the end of the first six books Tom is expelled in disgrace, Allworthy is comprehensively duped, and Sophia is threatened with forced marriage to Blifil, which would indeed be a fate worse than death. These events precipitate Tom's first adult crisis of conscience—what to do about the love between himself and Sophia. His decision to leave Sophia shows that if his worldly education by Square and Thwackum has been deficient, his moral education by Allworthy has been exemplary. From the moment he becomes aware of his own feelings, and that they are returned, his conflict begins:

> if he could hope to find no Bar to his Happiness from the Daughter, he thought himself certain of meeting an effectual Bar in the Father; who, though he was a Country Squire in his Diversions, was perfectly a Man of the World in whatever regarded his Fortune. (V, iii; 221)

Tom might have eloped, as Fielding did with Charlotte, but:

> As he had therefore no Hopes of obtaining her Father's Consent, so he thought to endeavour to succeed without it, and by such Means to frustrate the Great Point of Mr. *Western's* Life, was to make a very ill Use of his Hospitality, and a very ungrateful Return to the many little Favours received (however roughly) at his Hands. (221)

And he realizes that Allworthy would absolutely disapprove, that: 'the least Attempt of such a Kind would make the sight of the guilty Person for ever odious to his Eyes' (221). Not surprisingly, Tom finds the conflict impossible to resolve while the relationship is secret, and the lovers are thrown into one another's company:

> He often resolved, in the Absence of *Sophia*, to leave her Father's House, and to see her no more; and as often, in her Presence, forgot all those Resolutions, and determined to pursue her at the Hazard of his

Life, and at the Forfeiture of what was much dearer to him. (V, vi; 235)

When the relationship becomes known, and opposed, and when Tom, partly as a result, has been turned away, he can no longer afford the luxury of indecision, and has to choose either to depart alone, or to try to persuade Sophia to join him. In addition he is goaded by the knowledge of Blifil's suit to Sophia. His final decision is described in this paragraph:

> The Thoughts of leaving her almost rent his Heart asunder; but the Consideration of reducing her to Ruin and Beggary still racked him, if possible, more; and if the violent Desire of possessing her Person could have induced him to listen one Moment to this Alternative, still he was by no means certain of her Resolution to indulge his Wishes at so high an Expence. The Resentment of Mr. *Allworthy*, and the Injury he must do to his Quiet, argued strongly against this latter; and lastly, the apparent Impossibility of his Success, even if he would sacrifice all these Considerations to it, came to his Assistance; and thus Honour at last, backed with Despair, with Gratitude to his Benefactor, and with real Love to his Mistress, got the better of burning Desire, and he resolved rather to quit *Sophia*, than to pursue her to her Ruin. (VI, xii; 312)

Tom's motivation is here described in the formal, abstract manner that the author customarily uses when his characters have conflicting desires. What is noticeably absent is the ironic revelation of real motives behind pretended ones, the usual technique when depicting the motivation of a Blifil or a Black George. Tom's violent desire to possess Sophia's person is bluntly called what it is, suggesting that Tom is honest with himself, a fact which immediately distinguishes him from most of the other people in the book. The image of abstract forces such as desire, despair, gratitude, and love competing for Tom's allegiance like lawyers arguing in court is common in Fielding. He does not follow the continuous flux of thought and feeling in the minds of his characters. Instead he marshalls the opposing motives into a formal conflict which is then described in summary form, and from a distance. Dr Johnson compared this method of characterization unfavourably with Richardson's closer attention to the mind in process:

> there was as great a difference between them as between a man who knew how a watch was made, and a man who could tell the hour by looking on the dial-plate.[26]

[26] Paulson and Lockwood (eds), *Henry Fielding: The Critical Heritage*, p. 438.

Fielding does not describe what happens in the minds of his characters in any great detail. He is not much concerned with those inner psychological dramas which have formed a staple of fiction from Richardson to Proust and Virginia Woolf. Unlike these novelists, whose gaze is directed inwards, Fielding looks out at other people whose inner lives are unknown, as indeed they are in life, and attempts to describe how their motives may be deduced from their actions. To judge the behaviour and hence the character of such people accurately is an important part of the wisdom *Tom Jones* celebrates. It is a guidebook to the motives of others rather than a *vade mecum* to the self. However interesting the construction of watches may be, when we look at one we usually want no more than to know the time. If it tells us that correctly, we assume that its inner workings are in order.

Fielding is a comic novelist, and a comic novelist is concerned with surfaces, with the social appearances that characters offer to the world. His typical method of characterization is to show the appearance a character tries to present to the world, and then to puncture this pretence by revealing what really lies underneath the mask. The comedy results from the revelation of hypocrisy and affectation, from the exposure of the truth behind the carefully maintained illusion, and of the real, ignoble motive behind the pretended, noble motive. The method works best when it is dealing with plausible hypocrites. It is less effective with characters like Tom, who have nothing to hide, and therefore nothing to be exposed by the author. The result is a certain flatness in passages like the one quoted. On the positive side, however, there is Tom's unselfish decision to sacrifice his own desires to Sophia's well-being. The author's strong endorsement of this decision is evident in his unironic use of the word 'honour'. The passage also generates a real sense of the intense conflict in Tom's mind, despite the inevitability of his choice. The result of all this is that Tom emerges as simpler than the characters exposed as vicious by the author, but also, paradoxically, more three-dimensional, more fully human in his commitment to people, not self-interest. Self-interest is a cold, bloodless taskmaster, whose disciples lack a fully human dimension for all their manipulative skill over those more human than themselves. The strength and worth of Tom's feelings endear him to us, even if their depiction is unsubtle, and at times a little wooden.

Tom chooses to leave Sophia immediately after he has been expelled by Allworthy. He is thus separated from the only two people he loves, the only two people of real worth in his early environment, and the only people who might protect him from his own weakness and a hostile world. By the end of the first six books, the first two volumes of the original six, Tom has been disowned by his mother, discriminated against by his tutors and the household, beaten repeatedly by Thwackum, betrayed and vilified by Blifil, ducked in the canal and had his arm broken in the service of Sophia, robbed of his only means of support by Black George, the main recipient of his generosity, duped by Molly, dismissed by Allworthy, abused unmercifully, and undeservedly, by Western, and cheated of his inheritance by Blifil. When he leaves Paradise Hall, and graduates from the academy of Thwackum to the university of hard knocks, his education, with which the first six books are concerned, has been punishingly comprehensive. It has not, however, altered his nature, or jaundiced his view of the world. His temper, we are later told, 'was naturally sanguine', and a sanguine temper 'puts us, in a Manner, out of the Reach of Fortune, and makes us happy without her Assistance' (XIII, vi; 708). Together with his irrepressible flow of good-humoured animal spirits, this temper enables Tom to judge human nature by the best examples of it he encounters, and not to trouble himself unduly about the misfortunes to which he is subjected by the worst. If this attitude lends some support to the opinion that Tom is ineducable, it also supports the contrary principle enunciated at the beginning of *Joseph Andrews* that example works more forcibly on the mind than precept, and that the example of an Allworthy and a Sophia can inspire the essentially good like Tom to realize the best in their natures.

While Tom has thus been getting wisdom, the reader has been introduced to the principal characters, the major themes, and the art of fiction on which *Tom Jones* is based. The first six books take place in the comparative tranquillity of the country where, though action is not lacking, there is a static, leisurely, pastoral quality, epitomized in the courtship of Tom and Sophia. When Tom sets off on his journey to London, to be followed by Sophia and the other main characters, the pace accelerates, although intermittently, and the action diffuses. Tom is adult, if not yet mature, and the long years of childhood are over. The forces of evil, which have harassed him throughout his childhood, have gathered themselves to try to destroy him. He is separated from the models of probity and wisdom who have guided him. For most of the rest of the book he is on his own, sometimes protected by his virtues, sometimes ensnared by imprudence and the schemes of wilier heads than his. But if the child is father to the man, and if the reader understands the author's obvious affection for his hero, he seems likely to turn out well.

Chapter Two

In Book Seven *Tom Jones* takes to the road, and for the next six books the scene shifts as we follow Tom and Sophia on their separate but intersecting journeys from Somerset to London. For the title page of the book Fielding chose the epigraph *Mores hominum multorum vidit*, in which Horace describes the comprehensive experience of Odysseus in the *Odyssey*: 'he viewed the customs of many people'. Dr Johnson was to begin *The Vanity of Human Wishes* with a similar sentiment:

> Let Observation with extensive View,
> Survey Mankind from *China* to *Peru*.[1]

If Fielding's survey of mankind in the central third of *Tom Jones* is geographically less extensive, it is no less ambitious. In the course of their journeying Tom and Sophia meet a cross-section of contemporary English society and they are thrown on their own resources to be tested, to learn, and to gain experience in the world outside their homes. The society they encounter represents mankind, at least in its essential features, since, as The Man of the Hill suggests after his travels, and as the eighteenth century believed, 'Human Nature is every where the same' (VIII, xv; 482). By comparison with the travels of The Man of the Hill, or of Odysseus, the journeys of Tom and Sophia are short, in distance and duration, but they are nonetheless epic. The author makes this clear in his choice of an epigraph, in his invocation of the Muse of Homer, Virgil, and Milton (XIII, i; 683), and in his claim that: '*Homer* and *Milton* . . . though they added the Ornament of Numbers to their Works, were both Historians of our Order' (IX, i; 492). Homer described the many and

---

[1] J. D. Fleeman (ed.), *Samuel Johnson: The Complete English Poems*, Harmondsworth 1971, p. 83.

various encounters of Odysseus' protracted travels, while Milton focused his attention on the battle between good and evil for the allegiance of Adam and Eve, but they shared the ambitious attempt to portray the essential nature of human experience for all men in all societies, and it is this that the author of *Tom Jones* seeks to emulate, in his own individual way. There are some obvious similarities. Tom, like Telemachus, and like the later Stephen Dedalus in Joyce's *Ulysses*, is in search of his father. The father may be an actual father, like Mr Summer or Ulysses, a spiritual father like Allworthy or Bloom, or a divine father, like Milton's God. Tom has been expelled from Paradise Hall, as Adam was expelled from Paradise, and both are seeking to discover that 'paradise within' that makes life liveable in a corrupted world, as well as seeking an ultimate reconciliation with the father who expelled them. When Tom is turned out by Allworthy, '*The World*', the author says:

> as *Milton* phrases it, *lay all before him*; and *Jones*, no more than *Adam*, had any Man to whom he might resort for Comfort or Assistance. (VII, ii; 331)

They are both, that is, immersed in the human flux of the world, and alienated from the providence which has so far watched over them.

One significant departure from the epic is the relative absence of warfare. *Tom Jones* is a quest epic, like the *Odyssey*, not a siege epic, like the *Iliad*, but even in the former there was considerable emphasis on martial prowess, and military or other fighting was the order of the day. Milton, it is true, challenged this emphasis:

> Not sedulous by Nature to indite
> Warrs, hitherto the onely Argument
> Heroic deemd, chief maistrie to dissect
> With long and tedious havoc fabl'd Knights
> In Battels feignd; the better fortitude
> Of Patience and Heroic Martyrdom
> Unsung.   (IX, 27–33)[2]

But even Milton devoted a book and a half of *Paradise Lost* to the war in Heaven. Fielding retains some of the paraphernalia of warfare in his mock-epic treatment of episodes like Molly's churchyard battle (IV, viii) and the Upton banquet (IX, v), but Tom has only the briefest of flirtations with real army life. He sets out for Bristol to go to sea and

---

[2] Helen Darbishire (ed.), *The Poetical Works of John Milton*, London 1958, p. 183.

chances across a party of soldiers making their way north to join the Duke of Cumberland's campaign to put down the Jacobite uprising of 1745. Tom's courage is never in question; indeed it is one of his distinguishing qualities, and he is a firm supporter of the Protestant religion, and hence of the Hanoverian cause (VII, xii; 374), but his skirmish with the army is short-lived. He fights Ensign Northerton not the rebels, and he gives up military life as unconcernedly as he had taken it on. Fielding himself was energetic and unequivocal in his support for the Hanoverian side in *The True Patriot* (1745–6) and *The Jacobite's Journal* (1747–8), and he praised the Duke of Cumberland, despite his bloody suppression of the rebel clans after the battle of Culloden, but he had little admiration for military adventurers, however famous, as he made clear in *Jonathan Wild*:

> In the histories of Alexander and Caesar we are frequently, and indeed impertinently, reminded of their benevolence and generosity, of their clemency and kindness. When the former had with fire and sword overrun a vast empire, had destroyed the lives of an immense number of innocent wretches, had scattered ruin and desolation like a whirlwind, we are told, as an example of his clemency, that he did not cut the throat of an old woman, and ravish her daughters, but was content with only undoing them. And when the mighty Caesar, with wonderful greatness of mind, had destroyed the liberties of his country, and with all the means of fraud and force had placed himself at the head of his equals, had corrupted and enslaved the greatest people whom the sun ever saw, we are reminded, as an evidence of his generosity, of his largesses to his followers and tools, by whose means he had accomplished his purpose, and by whose assistance he was to establish it.[3]

We can expect little glorification of war from the man who wrote that, and Tom's military exploits in fact constitute only a brief episode among many others, and he sees no actual fighting. The episode is not, however, unimportant in the development of Tom's character. Disappointed lovers often go off to the wars, but Tom, though genuinely grieved by the loss of Sophia, is no gloomy Vronsky hell-bent on self-destruction. Tom may have lost his mistress, at least for the present, and something of his peace of mind, but he retains his sanguine temper. He enters into the spirit of things with the soldiers; indeed he enters too far into it, making two important errors of judgement, which will obstruct his reconciliation to Allworthy, and his reunion with Sophia.

---

[3] *Jonathan Wild*, I, i; Henley, Vol. II, p. 3.

The first of these is his yielding to the insistence of the lieutenant that he name the mistress he has toasted. Tom is later to pay dearly for Partridge's misuse of Sophia's name in the kitchens of inns, but on this first occasion he is himself guilty of a serious indiscretion in exposing her name to the lewd aspersions of Ensign Northerton. Tom tries to rectify his mistake by defending his mistress, and receives a bottle in the head for his trouble. The upshot of this squalid bar-room fight is Tom's attempt to uphold his honour by duelling with Northerton. He decides on this duel only after a conflict of conscience in which he chooses the wrong, though socially approved course of action. The conflicting attitudes emerge in a long debate he has with the lieutenant, who commends his religious sentiments, except as they apply to honour, which the lieutenant maintains a soldier must uphold:

No, no, my dear Boy, be a good Christian as long as you live; but be a Man of Honour too, and never put up an Affront; not all the Books, nor all the Parsons in the World, shall ever persuade me to that. (VII, xiii; 384)

Tom is not entirely persuaded, but he decides, with an unquiet conscience, to seek out Northerton at once, and to fight him. He is saved from carrying out this intention by Northerton's flight from custody, and serious consequences are thus avoided, but Tom's mistaken notions of honour in love and war are to lead to his two most disreputable, and potentially disastrous, encounters, with Lady Bellaston and Mr Fitzpatrick, in the final section of the book.

The conflict with Northerton shows some of the ways in which the comic epic poem in prose differs from the serious verse epic. In the initial confrontation, Tom's cause, defending a slandered lady's honour, is noble enough, but being laid out with a bottle is not. It belongs rather to the low-life rough-and-tumble of the picaresque world, familiar to Fielding's readers in works like the Spanish *Lazarillo de Tormes* and the French *Gil Blas*, as well as in Defoe's English narratives. Northerton is a typical picaro in being a lower-class pretender to the rank of officer, in throwing a bottle at Tom without warning instead of waiting for a fair fight, and in avoiding a subsequent reckoning and saving his skin by bribing the landlady to release him from custody. The picaro was an amoral survivor in a dangerous world, with no leisure for moral scruples. Tom, who undergoes a conflict between religion and honour, is neither 'hero' nor picaro. When he later encounters Northerton attempting to rob and murder Mrs Waters, Tom has the satisfaction of giving him the drubbing he deserves with 'his trusty Oaken Stick' (IX, ii; 496). Such beatings, in which honour may be satisfied without blood being shed, are clearly more to the author's taste than potentially lethal duels.

The comic treatment of the Northerton episode is another indication that *Tom Jones* occupies a middle ground between the epic and the picaresque. The incidents are contrived so that they appear threatening, but have no serious consequences. The surgeon who treats Tom, for example, exaggerates the injury and his own importance. The reader quickly realizes that he is a fool, and that Tom is not seriously hurt. The finest comic touch is the description of the ghost-like Tom approaching the sentinel supposedly guarding Northerton:

> The Clock had now struck Twelve ... when *Jones* ... issued forth in Pursuit of his Enemy ... It is not easy to conceive a much more tremendous Figure than he now exhibited. He had on, as we have said, a light-coloured Coat, covered with Streams of Blood. His Face, which missed that very Blood, as well as twenty Ounces more drawn from him by the Surgeon, was pallid. Round his Head was a Quantity of Bandage, not unlike a Turban. In the right Hand he carried a Sword, and in the left a Candle. So that the bloody *Banquo* was not worthy to be compared to him. In Fact, I believe a more dreadful Apparition was never raised in a Church-yard, nor in the Imagination of any good People met in a Winter Evening over a Christmas Fire in *Somersetshire*.
>
> When the Centinel first saw our Heroe approach, his Hair began gently to lift up his Grenadier Cap; and in the same Instant his Knees fell to Blows with each other. Presently his whole Body was seized with worse than an Ague Fit. He then fired his Piece, and fell flat on his Face.
>
> Whether Fear or Courage was the Occasion of his Firing, or whether he took Aim at the Object of his Terror, I cannot say. If he did, however, he had the good Fortune to miss his Man. (VII, xiv; 387–8)

The scene has tragic potential. Tom intends to challenge Northerton, and one of them might have been killed in the ensuing duel. Even the terrified sentinel, who fires his piece, might easily have shot someone. But the author's arch tone and his unconcerned elegance of phrasing convert the drama into high comedy. He creates the trappings of terror, but he places them in the theatre, with Banquo's ghost and with Tom turbaned like the Grand Turk in a mummer's play, and in the imaginations of the good people of Somerset (of whom the sentinel was perhaps one), rather than in Tom or the reader. The pictured winter's evening over a Christmas fire, reminiscent of *The Winter's Tale* (II, i; 25) and Milton's *L'Allegro*, suggests the telling of ghost stories in a warm and cosy setting, with the listeners enjoying a pleasurable frisson of terror. In this way the danger and excitement of Tom's mission is contained within a comic frame. The author's account of the sentinel's motives is typical of this containment. Having made it apparent that the sentinel is terrified, he pretends not to know whether fear or courage prompted his shot. In his next breath he admits, seemingly accidentally, that it was in fact fear, adding that the sentinel had the good fortune to miss his man. Tom is also fortunate in confronting so unmilitary a sentinel whose shot is wide of the mark either because he omitted to take aim or because he was trembling too much to shoot straight. Much of the comedy of *Tom Jones* is built on such calculated discrepancies between what is said and what is conveyed, and when this method is applied to a situation which ought to be serious but is made hilarious the result is doubly comic.

While Tom is thus engaged with Northerton and the army, Sophia is fighting her own battles at home. Book Seven sees a major development of her character, which centres on her family's attempts to marry her to Blifil. Sophia refuses to comply with their wishes and eventually is obliged to leave home to avoid the match. Her decision to run away from home is the most important she has to make, matching Tom's decision to leave her rather than to ruin her fortunes, and we see more of her while she is making it than at any other stage of the book. Before she decides to leave she is sorely tested by her father and her aunt. Though she has herself never married, Di Western is not at all reluctant to proffer advice to her niece on the nature and purposes of marriage:

> she proceeded to read her a long Lecture on the Subject of Matrimony; which she treated not as a romantic Scheme of Happiness arising from Love, as it hath been described by the Poets; nor did she mention any of those Purposes for which we are taught by Divines to regard it as instituted by sacred Authority; she considered it rather as a Fund in which prudent Women deposite their Fortunes to the best Advantage, in order to receive a larger Interest for them, than they could have elsewhere. (VII, iii; 332)

There are a number of key words in this passage which the reader of *Tom Jones* has by this time been alerted to treat with caution if not suspicion: words like prudent, advantage, and interest are tainted by their association with the Blifils of the world, who prudently consult their own interest, and look to their advantage, at the expense of more generous behaviour. And any long lecture, even if it is given by Allworthy, is likely to be misdirected, or pompous, or both. In this instance, the lecture may be contrasted with Sophia's succinct objection to the match: ' "A very solid Objection, in my Opinion," says *Sophia*,—"I hate him" ' (333). The author has already implied that he disagrees with the worldly views of Mrs Western by citing the very different concepts of marriage espoused by poets and divines. The debate between aunt and niece contrasts the true wisdom of Sophia with its specious, worldly counterpart. The author blends the spirited dialogue with comments supporting Sophia's self-assertion and condemning the cruelty of her family. And to prevent the matter becoming solemn as well as serious, he adds a comic altercation between Western and his sister about the management of the match, which draws their joint fire away from Sophia and directs it at one another.

Sophia fails to exploit the respite this gives her—as the author suggests a more worldly woman would—by taking sides and playing up the dissension. When Mrs Western stalks off in a rage, Sophia omits to compliment her father at the expense of her aunt:

> poor *Sophia* was all Simplicity. By which Word we do not intend to insinuate to the Reader, that she was silly, which is generally understood as a synonimous Term with simple: For she was indeed a most sensible Girl, and her Understanding was of the first Rate; but she wanted that useful Art which Females convert to so many good Purposes in Life, and which, as it rather arises from the Heart, than from the Head, is often the Property of the silliest of Women. (VII, iii; 337–8)

As a result of her failure to exploit the situation to her own advantage, Sophia is treated to a tirade from her father urging her to marry Blifil. The author takes the opportunity to insert a brief history of Western's own marriage, which, like the one he is trying to force upon his daughter, was an arranged match prompted solely by financial motives. Both Western and his wife were miserable, living separate and isolated lives devoid of love. Sophia, who refused to take sides there also, has had ample opportunity to observe at close hand the results of a loveless marriage and is determined not to marry a man she hates.

As the scene develops it becomes apparent that, despite the previously quoted comment, she is not entirely without guile. She sets in progress a reconciliation between her father and her aunt with a judiciously directed comment to her father:

'if my Aunt had died Yesterday, I am convinced she would have left you her whole Fortune.'

Whether *Sophia* intended it or no, I shall not presume to assert; but certain it is, these last Words penetrated very deep into the Ears of her Father, and produced a much more sensible Effect than all she had said before. He received the Sound with much the same Action as a Man receives a Bullet in his Head. (VII, v; 341)

Whenever the author pretends not to know the motives of his characters, he has already made it plain to the reader what those motives are. The real difference between this calculation and Sophia's earlier simplicity is that in the earlier case she would have aggravated the conflict to ease her own situation, whereas here she reconciles brother and sister, with the eventual result that they will again unite against her. Her concern is for her father and her aunt, not for herself. Which is not to say that she does not have a proper regard for her own essential interests, as she displays in her firmly maintained resistance to a match she knows would make her miserable for life. Later in the conflict she is momentarily tempted to make a sacrifice of herself to the wishes of her father. The author describes this temptation much as George Eliot was to describe, at considerably greater length, Dorothea's passion for self-sacrifice in *Middlemarch*. Sophia, however, has the good sense to reject the temptation:

The Idea, therefore, of the immense Happiness she should convey to her Father by her Consent to this Match, made a strong Impression on her Mind. Again, the extreme Piety of such an Act of Obedience, worked very forcibly, as she had a very deep Sense of Religion. Lastly, when she reflected how much she herself was to suffer, being indeed to become little less than a Sacrifice, or a Martyr, to filial Love and Duty, she felt an agreeable Tickling in a certain little Passion, which tho' it bears no immediate Affinity either to Religion or Virtue, is often so kind as to lend great Assistance in executing the Purposes of both. (VII, ix; 360)

The 'certain little passion' is pride, which not only bears no immediate affinity to religion or virtue, but is in fact the first of the seven deadly sins. If Sophia is human enough to feel a passing attraction for self-sacrifice, she has sound human motives for quickly rejecting it:

the Thoughts of her beloved *Jones*, and some Hopes (however distant) in which he was very particularly concerned, immediately destroyed all which filial Love, Piety and Pride had, with their joint Endeavours, been labouring to bring about. (361)

Sophia, the book's model of wisdom, is prompted by very human passions, and not by the inhuman theorizing of Square, Thwackum and Mrs Western. The author makes this particularly clear by unobtrusively including 'Pride' as the motive he had earlier left the reader to ascertain for himself. *Tom Jones* is full of such exercises designed to test the reader's attention to the text.

Sophia now faces the threat of being forced to marry Blifil. Tom is gone, and her family are united against her. Even Allworthy, who if he knew the real situation would forbid all coercion, is so deceived about Blifil's feelings, and Sophia's objection, that he supports the match. At this suspenseful moment the author abruptly takes leave of his heroine, and returns to Tom's adventures on the road. The Northerton episode, already considered, is narrated. Book Eight then begins with a discussion of the place of 'the Marvellous' in fiction. Such sudden changes of direction form an important part of the art of contrast in *Tom Jones*, particularly in the middle third of the book. Whenever the reader's gaze becomes too intently fixed on threatening events, he is whisked away to another part of the story, or to a discussion of the art of fiction. On the one hand this heightens the suspense, while on the other it shows the author unconcerned, and so reduces the tension. The luxury of suspending disbelief, and abandoning oneself to the fictional illusion, is allowed only sparingly in this work. The art of fiction it exemplifies combines the pleasures of imaginative involvement with the responsibilities of judgement. Like Brecht, the author captures our imagination only with the purpose of returning us to the real world better able to judge it correctly.

The discussion of 'the Marvellous' illustrates this theory of fiction. The author suggests that: 'it may very reasonably be required of every Writer, that he keeps within the Bounds of Possibility' (VIII, i; 396–7). He further distinguishes his epic from Homer's by arguing that Homer relied too heavily on divine characters. Had he limited his use of supernatural agents, as Horace was to argue all writers should:

> We should not then have seen his Gods coming on trivial Errands, and often behaving themselves so as not only to forfeit all Title to Respect, but to become the Objects of Scorn and Derision. (398)

The author does allow modern writers the use of ghosts, but as the incident of the sentinel, which immediately precedes this chapter, illustrates, he himself has not much belief in them:

nor would I advise the Introduction of them at all in those Works, or by those Authors to which, or to whom a Horse-Laugh in the Reader, would be any great Prejudice or Mortification. (399)

But the Marvellous is not ruled out of modern fiction along with the supernatural. The marvellous which the author does allow is the portrayal of what Aristotle calls the improbable possibility:

> if the Historian will confine himself to what really happened, and utterly reject any Circumstance, which, tho' never so well attested, he must be well assured is false, he will sometimes fall into the Marvellous, but never into the Incredible. (401-2)

To illustrate his point, the author cites two true but improbable examples from contemporary history. The appalling ingratitude of Mr Fisher, who murdered his friend and generous benefactor brutally and without remorse, is improbably evil. It is contrasted to the outstanding public and private virtue of Ralph Allen, which is so improbably good that few readers would believe it existed outside the author's imagination. The judicious writer, then, 'will confine himself within the Bounds of Probability'; but:

> it is by no means necessary that his Characters, or his Incidents, should be trite, common, or vulgar; such as happen in every Street, or in every House, or which may be met with in the home Articles of a Newspaper. Nor must he be inhibited from shewing many Persons and Things, which may possibly have never fallen within the Knowledge of great Part of his Readers. (406-7)

The entire thrust of this chapter is summed up in a brief comment in the middle of the Northerton affair:

> it is our Business to relate Facts as they are; which when we have done, it is the Part of the learned and sagacious Reader to consult that original Book of Nature, whence every Passage in our Work is transcribed, tho' we quote not always the particular Page for its Authority. (VII, xii; 377)

On this basic principle the author rests his case: his work is true to the book of nature, divinely ordained as the Bible is divinely inspired, and it is on that firm basis of truth that its claim to the reader's attention is founded. The other literary forms to which the author refers, and from which he borrows, are models for *Tom Jones* only in this essential sense, that they also truly portray human nature. Their other qualities are ornamental, peripheral, incidental, and may be dismissed, ignored, or laughed at in parody by the author of *Tom Jones*.

With the form of his work thus further clarified, the author returns to the exploits of his hero. As Tom's journey continues he is joined by Partridge, who denies the common rumour that he is Tom's father but decides to travel with him. The most important of their encounters in this part of the narrative is with The Man of the Hill. Tom and Partridge seek shelter in his house, and Tom saves him from being robbed at his own door. The Man of the Hill then tells the story of his life to his guests. It is a sorry tale of youth dissipated at Oxford and the gaming tables of London, of betrayals by mistress and friends, of repentance followed by extensive, unrewarding travel, and finally of thirty years of withdrawal and isolation from human contact. These experiences have made him something of a philosopher, and he is religious in the monkish sense of admiring God's creation while avoiding his fellow man. Much of what he says is the stock-in-trade of satirists and his alienation from human society recalls that of Gulliver at the end of his travels or the hermit in *Rasselas*. His misanthropy and seclusion serve as a contrast to Tom's ready involvement with others, and his wasted youth shows up Tom's basic good sense in avoiding evil, if not imprudent, behaviour. In his convincing refutation of The Man of the Hill's misanthropy, Tom reveals a more thoughtful strain than has yet appeared:

> you here fall into an Error, which, in my little Experience, I have observed to be a very common one, by taking the Character of Mankind from the worst and basest among them; whereas indeed, as an excellent Writer observes, nothing should be esteemed as characteristical of a Species, but what is to be found among the best and most perfect Individuals of that Species. This Error, I believe, is generally committed by those who, from Want of proper Caution in the Choice of their Friends and Acquaintance, have suffered Injuries from bad and worthless Men; two or three Instances of which are very unjustly charged on all Human Nature. (VIII, xv; 485)

When The Man of the Hill protests that his first mistress and his first friend betrayed him, Tom answers, tellingly: 'What better, my good Sir, could be expected in Love derived from the Stews, or in Friendship first produced and nourished at the Gaming-Table!' (485). While the author's view of the truth lies somewhere between Tom's confidence in the best of the species, and The Man of the Hill's suspicion of all of the species, he certainly endorses Tom's rejection of misanthropy and withdrawal as responses to the all too prevalent evil in the world. Fielding like Shaftesbury preferred a philosophy of action and involvement in the affairs of the world to one of inaction and retreat.[4] A practical demonstration of the difference between the two views follows the next morning, when the party hears the screams of Mrs Waters, about to be murdered by Northerton. Tom immediately runs to the rescue, 'without the least Apprehension or Concern for his own Safety' (495), while his host: 'sat himself down on the Brow, where, tho' he had a Gun in his Hand, he with great Patience and Unconcern... attended the Issue' (IX, ii; 497). Had Tom behaved so when The Man of the Hill was attacked the previous night, the Man might have been killed, but even that does not prompt him to help the unarmed Tom to rescue another victim. In other circumstances, Tom's ready response to the needs of others has landed him in trouble, but the virtue of this readiness is frequently demonstrated in the middle third of the book, when he rescues more than one victim from imminent peril.

Mrs Waters, the victim on this occasion, is no hater of men, and the warmth of her gratitude to her rescuer is in marked contrast to the cold indifference of The Man of the Hill. Tom, whom we have just seen delivering admirable sentiments, is led into his second sexual escapade by this warmth, which finds a ready response in his own. The relationship develops at the inn at Upton, to which Tom escorts Mrs Waters. The Upton scenes which include this affair form the structural centre of *Tom Jones*. They occur at the physical centre of the work, the mid-point of the journeys to London, and the point at which Sophia overtakes Tom, and becomes the pursued and not the pursuer. They are enclosed on either side by the comparatively static narratives of The Man of the Hill and Mrs Fitzpatrick. Fielding's celebrated plotting is nowhere more evident than here, where the many narrative threads of the book meet and cross, and his invention of comic incident is amply demonstrated in a furious sequence of events.[5] In a dazzling display of virtuosity, characters enter and leave at brief intervals, there are arguments and all-in fights, bedrooms are broken into as a result of mistaken identities, embarrassing

---

[4] See Stanley Grean, *Shaftesbury's Philosophy of Religion and Ethics*, Ohio University Press 1967, p. 7.

[5] On the symmetrical structure of the book see Frederick W. Hilles, 'Art and Artifice in *Tom Jones*' in Maynard Mack and Ian Gregor (eds), *Imagined Worlds*, London 1968, pp. 91–110.

meetings take place, and, poignantly, the hero and heroine spend some hours under the same roof without meeting. This is all accomplished with stylistic finesse and great good-humour, which help to make the Upton sequence one of the high points of *Tom Jones*.

The action opens with the arrival of Tom and Mrs Waters at the inn, the description of which sets the tone for what is to follow. It has been preceded by the progress of Tom and Mrs Waters from Mazard Hill to Upton, Mrs Waters with her bosom exposed, as a result of her struggle with Northerton, and Tom marching in front to save her, as he thinks, from embarrassment:

> But tho' I cannot believe that *Jones* was designedly tempted by his Fair One to look behind him, yet as she frequently wanted his Assistance to help her over Stiles, and had besides many Trips and other Accidents, he was often obliged to turn about. However, he had better Fortune than what attended poor *Orpheus*; for he brought his Companion, or rather Follower, safe into the famous Town of *Upton*. (IX, ii; 498–9)

The temptation is to continue, and so is the mock-heroic elaboration of the author. Robert Alter reckons that the description of the Upton landlady's reception of the two travellers, which takes some four hundred words, would probably have taken Smollett thirty-five.[6] The commentary is not merely ornamental, however, as it serves a number of the author's purposes. He has to describe a brawl, and a casual sexual adventure, neither of which reflects much credit on his hero. He therefore chooses an artificial, mock-heroic manner, which can convert a potentially squalid sequence into high comedy, and can predispose the reader to be tolerant rather than censorious, and amused rather than indignant. The tone is brilliantly managed:

> Our Travellers had happened to take up their Residence at a House of exceeding good Repute, whither *Irish* Ladies of strict Virtue, and many Northern Lasses of the same Predicament, were accustomed to resort in their Way to *Bath*. (IX, iii; 500)

The insertion of 'predicament' into this passage explodes the hypocrisy of the landlady and her guests, for whom virtue is indeed a predicament, from which they hope to escape in the newly-fashionable resort of Bath. The 'exceeding good Repute' of the house is something of a euphemism:

---

[6] *Rogue's Progress: Studies in the Picaresque Novel*, Cambridge, Mass. 1965, p. 85.

Not that I would intimate, that such strict Chastity as was preserved in the Temple of *Vesta* can possibly be maintained at a public Inn. My good Landlady did not hope for such a Blessing, nor would any of the Ladies I have spoken of. (500)

Though she professes otherwise, the real reason the landlady objects to Tom and Mrs Waters is their appearance of ragged poverty, and not:

Purposes in their Intention, which, tho' tolerated in some Christian Countries, connived at in others, and practised in all; are however as expressly forbidden as Murder, or any other horrid Vice, by that Religion which is universally believed in those Countries. (500)

This neatly encapsulates the larger hypocrisy of an entire culture, which takes Scripture as its warrant for condemning both adultery and murder but which is actually so much more tolerant of the former as virtually to condone it. The real belief, which, though not professed, is universally practised, is that adultery is less vicious and less injurious to society than murder. Tom has his sexual lapses, but he does not kill anyone, and when he risks doing so by duelling the consequences are more threatening than the real but less sobering consequences of his affairs with Molly, Mrs Waters and Lady Bellaston.

Tom's affair with Mrs Waters at Upton further clarifies the author's views on sexual behaviour, which have already been discussed with reference to Molly and Sophia. It is important not to misunderstand his judgement on this vexed moral question. He does not secretly condone or surreptitiously admire Tom's sexual adventures. Compared to Tom's real love for Sophia, they are poor substitutes indeed. That they are better, more natural substitutes than Blifil's self-satisfaction, does not elevate them very highly in the author's moral scale. On the other hand Tom is young, vigorous, attractive to women, and inclined to behave as others wish him to rather more than he should. In all his affairs the women are the initiators, and the author's view of such mutually satisfying encounters is humanly tolerant, though morally disapproving.[7] The plot is so managed that Tom suffers for his lapses, and learns from them how to distinguish between love and physical gratification. The author defends Tom, but not because he has done no wrong. He defends him from the hypocritically virtuous who pretend that sexual sins are the deadliest, the

---

[7] John Middleton Murry discusses this aspect of the book perceptively in 'Fielding's "Sexual Ethic"' in *Tom Jones* in Ronald Paulson (ed.), *Fielding: A Collection of Critical Essays*, Englewood Cliffs 1962, pp. 89–97.

least forgivable, and who are only too willing to cast stones at adulterers. He would suggest, as Christ did, that they should first look into their own hearts, and seek out the true source of their murderous indignation.

All of this is lightly done in the Upton sequence, particularly in the seduction scene itself (IX, v), which is its centrepiece, and one of the most brilliantly rendered scenes in Fielding. It must have been a difficult scene for the author, because he had to show Tom succumbing to the comfortable Mrs Waters without altogether betraying his love for Sophia. It is Tom's physical appetite that mutinies at Upton. He first satisfies his hunger with a plentiful meal, and his appetite is compared to Ulysses' in 'that eating Poem of the Odyssey'. Ulysses had his share of sexual as well as gastronomic adventures, and when the author speaks of Tom laying about with 'immoderate Ardour' at the table, he is describing his sexual appetite as well as his hunger. Tom's sexual appetite does not, however, respond to the enticements of Mrs Waters, or even notice them, until his hunger has been satisfied, which suggests that his interest in her is confined to physical appetite.

The point of view then shifts to Mrs Waters. Tom is described, through her passion-inflamed eyes, as a combination of Hercules and Adonis:

> When the Reader hath duly reflected on these many Charms which all centered in our Heroe, and considers at the same Time the fresh Obligations which Mrs. *Waters* had to him, it will be a Mark more of Prudery than Candour to entertain a bad Opinion of her, because she conceived a very good Opinion of him. (510)

This expertly manoeuvres the reader into a tolerant frame of mind for the amorous battle which is to follow. It is introduced with a mock-Miltonic invocation as 'a Description hitherto unessayed either in Prose or Verse' (511), and the epic manner is maintained throughout the following scene, in which Mrs Waters lays on with ogles and sighs, but Tom is initially protected by his loyalty to the God of Eating. Only when this newly-invented deity has been copiously propitiated does Tom fall victim to the whole artillery of love as discharged at him by his fair opponent. The traditional images of warfare are used to describe Mrs Waters' campaign, which culminates in victory:

> To confess the Truth, I am afraid Mr. *Jones* maintained a Kind of *Dutch* Defence, and treacherously delivered up the Garrison without duly weighing his Allegiance to the fair *Sophia*. In short, no sooner had the amorous Parley ended, and the Lady had unmasked the Royal

Battery, by carelessly letting her Handkerchief drop from her Neck, than the Heart of Mr. *Jones* was entirely taken. (513)

The dozens of solemn sonnets comparing love to a siege are here brilliantly parodied. The wider allusions to the epic world of Homer and Milton, and to Pasiphae and her bull, serve both to level Tom's behaviour with that of other heroes, and conversely to keep elevated, and therefore comic, a scene which might easily have become low. Later events in the book emphasize that Tom's succumbing to Mrs Waters was a significant moral lapse. Its casualness is punished by the threat of incest, and its slighting of Sophia is punished by her discovery of what happened and of Tom's supposed freedom with her name, which together alienate her affections. The essential honesty and naturalness of Tom's response, however, are rewarded by the absence of any lasting consequences. What happened at Upton was culpable, but it was human and credible. Tom is no paragon, no parody of human nature, like Pamela. Homer and nature were, Pope said, the same, and the heroes of Fielding, like the heroes of Homer, go the way of all flesh.

The pleasures of the flesh are notoriously brief, however, and Tom and Mrs Waters are rudely broken in upon, in the middle of the night, by an irate Mr Fitzpatrick in pursuit of his runaway wife, who is in fact staying in another room of the inn. A splendidly comic scene ensues, in which Mrs Waters protests that her reputation has been threatened by the simultaneous irruption into her bedroom of Fitzpatrick and companion and Jones, intent, to all appearances, on murder, robbery, and, most of all, rape. Having chosen the part 'of a modest Lady, who was awakened out of her Sleep by three strange Men in her Chamber', she executes it so well 'that none of our Theatrical Actresses could exceed her, in any of their Performances, either on or off the Stage' (X, ii; 532). From this incident the comic pace accelerates. Sophia and Mrs Honour arrive, learn of Tom's real freedoms with Mrs Waters and his supposed freedoms with Sophia's name, and depart, leaving Sophia's muff on Tom's bed. Mr Fitzpatrick again fails to find his wife, who has also left the inn. Squire Western arrives, and finding Tom attempts to take first physical and then legal vengeance on him, unsuccessfully. He then departs in pursuit of Sophia, as do Tom and Partridge, while Mrs Waters accompanies Mr Fitzpatrick to Bath.

After this furious burst of narrative action, which has reshaped the central relationships of the book and set in train the actions which are to control the second half of the narrative, the author slackens the pace with two retrospective narratives. The first, which he tells himself, recounts the events of Sophia's last day at home before fleeing from the arranged marriage with Blifil. Her courage, her spirit, and her ability to act determinedly and sensibly to secure her own happiness are all demonstrated. She does not languish under her father's ire, like Clarissa who waits at home until lured away by the seducer Lovelace. When the situation becomes intolerable, Sophia makes good her escape.

The second retrospective narrative is Mrs Fitzpatrick's story, which she tells to Sophia. The girls are cousins and had lived together for a time as children with Mrs Western. Harriet married an Irish fortune-hunter at Bath, who, like Mirabel in *The Way of the World*, pretended love to the aunt to gain access to the niece. Hers is an unsavoury story of greed, deception, gullibility, and exploitation. Like the story of The Man of the Hill, it reveals what it is like to live in a world peopled by Blifils, and devoid of Allworthys. The effect on Harriet of her experience has not been to make her withdraw from the world, but rather to throw herself into the illicit pleasures it offers with determined gusto. She is a creature of that world, and characterizes herself vividly, if unflatteringly, as she describes her adventures and misadventures in it. Sophia's response to her cousin's story, and her comments upon it, throw the two girls into clearly defined contrast. Harriet is giddy, unthinking, pleasure-seeking, and unrepentant. She fully lives up to her childhood name of Miss Giddy (XI, iv; 581). Sophia, by contrast, was known as Miss Graveairs. She is not exactly grave as she listens to Harriet's prattle, but she is aware of the moral shallowness of her cousin, and she comes to suspect that her relationship with the Irish lord is not the platonic friendship that Harriet maintains it to be. The author, as is his custom, has already informed the reader of the peer's part in Harriet's escape from her husband:

> To say Truth, it was by his Assistance, that she had been enabled to escape from her Husband; for this Nobleman had the same gallant Disposition with those renowned Knights, of whom we read in heroic Story, and had delivered many an imprisoned Nymph from Durance . . . I have often suspected that those very Enchanters with which Romance every where abounds, were in reality no other than the Husbands of those Days; and Matrimony itself was perhaps the enchanted Castle in which the Nymphs were said to be confined. (XI, viii; 607)

Harriet was an indefatigable reader, and she views her own story as the plot of a romance. The author conveys this amusingly in his parody, while suggesting that adulterous passion, the staple of romance, was the real motive for the nobleman's gallantry. The very term 'gallant' has been so debased by its use as a euphemism for adulterous that it immediately prompts a knowing smile.[8] Harriet omits all reference to the peer from her first account of her experiences, but Sophia has her suspicions, which are confirmed by the later meeting with the peer. The author chooses this point to distinguish between two kinds of suspicion, one arising from a bad heart, and the other from a wise head:

> I cannot help therefore regarding this vast Quicksightedness into Evil, as a vicious Excess, and as a very pernicious Evil in itself. And I am the more inclined to this Opinion, as I am afraid it always proceeds from a bad Heart, for the Reasons I have above-mentioned, and for one more, namely, because I never knew it the Property of a good one. Now from this Degree of Suspicion I entirely and absolutely acquit *Sophia*.
>
> A second Degree of this Quality seems to arise from the Head. This is indeed no other than the Faculty of seeing what is before your Eyes, and of drawing Conclusions from what you see ... of this Degree of Suspicion I believe *Sophia* was guilty. From this Degree of Suspicion she had, in Fact, conceived an Opinion, that her Cousin was really not better than she should be. (XI, x; 615–16)

The entire passage from which this quotation is taken is a crucial definition of the kind of suspicion proper to wisdom. This was a preoccupying concern for Fielding, who felt, as we have seen, that those who were simply good were too often easy prey for those who were not. Sophia, however, like the author, and he trusts, the reader, is wise as well as good. It is an unusual combination in one of Fielding's characters, and he takes trouble to define for the reader how Sophia may be good, and innocent, and yet perceive the evil in others. In an earlier passage he has made it clear that Tom does not have this wisdom though he may eventually learn it:

> As for *Jones*, he was well satisfied with the Truth of what the other had asserted, and believed that *Partridge* had no other Inducements but Love to him, and Zeal for the Cause. A blameable Want of Caution, and Diffidence in the Veracity of others, in which he was highly worthy of Censure. To say the Truth, there are but two Ways by which Men become possessed of this excellent Quality. The one is from long Experience, and the other is from Nature; which last, I presume, is often meant by Genius, or great natural Parts; and it is infinitely the

---

[8] See *OED*, gallant, A7, B3; and gallantry, 8. Cf. the description of Harriet Fitzpatrick's 'gallant' Irish lord (XI, viii; 607).

better of the two, not only as we are Masters of it much earlier in Life, but as it is much more infallible and conclusive ... As *Jones* had not this Gift from Nature, he was too young to have gained it by Experience. (VIII, vii; 427–8)

The author overstates Tom's fault in believing Partridge's professions too readily and clearly implies that Tom merits praise for his openness as well as censure for his credulity. Tom certainly lacks the vast quicksightedness into evil which leads Partridge to disbelieve Tom's story, to assume that Allworthy is Tom's father, and to interpret Allworthy's charity as: 'a kind of Smart-money, or ... Atonement for Injustice' (427). On the other hand he lacks Sophia's native perception, which might have led him to a true judgement of Partridge, and he is therefore condemned to toil in hope's delusive mine, until he learns, by slow experience, to think less well of men than his good-nature prompts him to think. This becomes possible only at the end of the book, when he is reunited with Sophia and Allworthy, and his lively impulses are tempered by his uncle's experience and his wife's wisdom.

Back at Upton, however, he is separated from Sophia and Allworthy and alienated from their affections. He is in the midst of his journey through the world, and has far to go and much to learn before he is reconciled to them. Sophia must also experience the world outside her home, both in her own journey and in her cousin's account of her marriage. The interpolated tales offer to these two characters what *Tom Jones* offers its readers, the chance to view imaginatively the pitfalls of inexperience, without having to suffer the consequences. The Man of the Hill and Mrs Fitzpatrick are coarser-grained than Tom and Sophia, and can participate fully in the picaresque world they describe, and so expose it thoroughly, from inside. Tom and Sophia, who are venturing into this world, are given timely insights into its darker areas, where, but for the grace of God, and their own good-nature, they might have gone. They are also able to show their true worth by disagreeing with the cynical views which their experiences have led The Man of the Hill and Mrs Fitzpatrick to adopt.

Both these narratives are told in the first person, in contrast to the third-person, authorial narration of the rest of *Tom Jones*. The author's deliberate use of contrast has already been discussed, and the interpolated narratives act as foils to the authorial narrative which surrounds them, a technique derived from Cervantes and the romances in which a newcomer is customarily invited to relate his 'history'. The presence of the benign, amusing author reassures the reader that the central trio will eventually overcome the pervasive hypocrisy and vice of their world, and when that presence is withdrawn the book ceases to be comic and darkens into picaresque. The Man of the Hill and Mrs Fitzpatrick describe a world that is squalid, petty, self-interested and amoral. Their struggle for survival seems familiar enough to the twentieth-century reader, used to a world in which God is dead, and man must make do as best he can.[9] The first-person narration is also familiar to modern readers, many of whom prefer it to the authorial narration of the rest of the work, which they feel pre-empts their own assessment of the fictional world by providing a ready-made judgement they feel forced to accept whether or not they agree with it. While this may be a legitimate complaint against some authorial narration, it is not so with Fielding's. The commentary in *Tom Jones* not only does not pre-empt the reader's judgement, but increases the demands made on that judgement to make its own assessment of character and incident. One only has to compare the quality of the writing of the Upton scenes with that of the two first-person narratives immediately before and after those scenes to see how superior Fielding's authorial narration is to his dramatic narration. The Upton scenes are alive with verve and gusto, with comic invention and stylistic bravura, with moral energy and *joie de vivre*. By comparison, the surrounding first-person narratives are drab. The narrators are as ordinary as their experiences, and the gain in authenticity which results from having them tell their own stories is more than offset by the loss of the author. The narratives are just long enough to give the reader a taste of another, tawdrier world and of another, drabber mode of narration than are to be found elsewhere in *Tom Jones*. Such visits to the infernal world of unrelieved egotism show up the virtues of generosity all the more brightly. And temporary separation from the guiding author shows how vital his presence is to the rest of the story. In his earlier work, Fielding experimented with different combinations of authorial and dramatic writing. He introduced authorial figures into several of his plays, and these were more popular with contemporary audiences, and remain more interesting, than his purely dramatic plays, where the characters speak entirely for themselves. He interpolated first-person narratives into all his fiction from *A Journey from This World to the Next* to *Amelia*, but, as in so many other instances, he seems to have got the combination right only in *Tom Jones* and to have misjudged it, to some extent, in his other work. The stories of The Man of the Hill and Mrs Fitzpatrick contrast refreshingly

---

[9] Claude Rawson draws a number of parallels between Fielding and representative modern writers in *Henry Fielding and the Augustan Ideal under Stress*.

with the rest of *Tom Jones*, without unduly interrupting its progress or diverting attention from its thematic concerns and artistic methods.[10]

When Tom eventually leaves Upton he is no longer wandering aimlessly but is resolved to pursue Sophia, and when he recovers her pocketbook and £100 note he has an excuse to see her again. Book Twelve is devoted to his experiences on the road to London, experiences which complete the central, peripatetic third of the work. The two episodes which will concern us here are the encounter with the gypsies, and the encounter with the travelling puppet-show. Tom is less morally engaged in these episodes than he had been at Upton and more of a picaresque spectator, but there are still moral lessons from which both he and the reader may profit.

The encounter with the gypsies is one of the most explicitly political episodes in *Tom Jones*.[11] While Tom and Partridge are travelling towards Coventry, their guide, who does not know the way himself, loses the party on a dirty byway in the middle of a storm. They eventually stumble across a barn inhabited by gypsies. Partridge, who is convinced that they have been bewitched, and that the gypsies are devils, is afraid to proceed, but Tom insists on taking refuge from the night and the storm in the barn. They find the gypsies celebrating a wedding:

> It is impossible to conceive a happier Set of People than appeared here to be met together. The utmost Mirth indeed shewed itself in every Countenance; nor was their Ball totally void of all Order and Decorum ... For these People are subject to a formal Government and Laws of their own, and all pay Obedience to one great Magistrate whom they call their King. (XII, xii; 667)

Tom quickly finds himself in the role of *ingénu*, like Gulliver, while the King explains the gypsy polity and his own position as a benevolent, absolute monarch. This discourse is, however, interrupted by the apprehension of Partridge and 'a young Female *Gypsy*' in amorous dalliance. The king demonstrates his qualities as a magistrate by quickly uncovering the truth of the situation, namely that the gypsy and her

---

[10] The best of many discussions of the two stories is Henry Knight Miller, 'The "Digressive" Tales in Fielding's *Tom Jones* and the Perspective of Romance', *Philological Quarterly*, Vol. 54, 1975, pp. 258–74.

[11] Martin C. Battestin discusses the political significance of the episode in 'Tom Jones and "His *Egyptian* Majesty": Fielding's Parable of Government', *PMLA*, Vol. LXXXII, 1967, pp. 68–77.

husband were conniving to entrap Partridge for money, and he punishes them and not Partridge. The punishment is shame, which the gypsies regard very seriously, unlike their English counterparts, who would not let shame deter them from vice nor regard it as a punishment. Tom is impressed: '*Jones* afterwards proceeded very gravely to sing forth the Happiness of those Subjects who live under such a Magistrate' (671). At this point the moral of the story, which Tom seems to endorse, appears to be that absolute rule, entrusted to such a man, is the best form of government. But the author steps in with a long comment explaining his views on the relative virtues of absolute monarchy and more limited forms of government, and he makes it clear that the story of the gypsies is a Swiftian parable, to be scrutinized by the reader for irony, not accepted at face value. Absolute monarchy is the best form of government, but only when the monarch is adequate to the office, which he seldom is. When he is not, the abuse of absolute power is as bad as the proper exercise of it is good. It is therefore wiser for a nation to choose a more limited form of government, which checks potential abuses of power more readily than an absolute system. The domestic implications of this for Fielding's contemporary readers were clear: they should not be seduced by the apparent attractions of an absolute Jacobite monarch, but should retain the more pragmatic and workable Hanoverian monarchy, which had been established deliberately to limit 'The Right Divine of Kings to govern wrong'.[12]

This long aside is interesting not only because of its relevance to contemporary politics, but also because it shows the author using his commentary to alert the reader to complexities implicit in seemingly straightforward narrative. Far from explaining the already obvious meaning of the narrative, as opponents of the authorial method sometimes claim he does, the author of *Tom Jones* uses the commentary to develop interpretations which the unaided reader might not readily perceive. In the present case Tom, whose heart is in the right place, and who is willing to fight for the Hanoverian cause, nonetheless lacks the maturity and experience to judge political systems with authority, and the real debate takes place between the author and the reader, not between Tom and the King.

Tom's encounter with the travelling puppet-show (XII, v–viii) makes its point more dramatically than the gypsy episode. Instead of the traditional entertainment of Punch and Joan, the puppet-show consists of

---

[12] *The Dunciad*, IV, 188; John Butt (ed.), *The Poems of Alexander Pope*, London 1963, p. 776.

'the fine and serious Part of the *Provok'd Husband*', a choice which meets with the approval of the audience, and is justified by the Master of the puppet-show as being 'calculated to improve the Morals of young People' (XII, v; 639). Tom, however, disagrees:

> I should have been glad to have seen my old Acquaintance Master *Punch* for all that; and so far from improving, I think, by leaving out him and his merry Wife *Joan*, you have spoiled your Puppet-show. (639)

On this occasion Tom is right, though he is a lone voice, until the author contrives some action to support his position, and to undermine the moral pretensions of the Master of the puppet-show and the rest of the audience. When the Master, urged on by the Clerk and the Exciseman, is in the midst of a harangue about the force of example, 'and how much the inferior Part of Mankind would be deterred from Vice, by observing how odious it was in their Superiors', he is interrupted by the discovery *in flagrante delicto* of his Merry-Andrew and the maid Grace, who pleads in her defence the example of the play:

> If I am a Wh--e ... my Betters are so as well as I. What was the fine Lady in the Puppet-show just now? I suppose she did not lie all Night out from her Husband for nothing. (641)

As so often in *Tom Jones*, the action neatly refutes the professions of the characters. The Master is further exposed two chapters later, when his Merry-Andrew responds to a beating with two damaging allegations:

> 'D--n your Bl--d, you Rascal,' says he, 'I have not only supported you, (for to me you owe all the Money you get) but I have saved you from the Gallows. Did you not want to rob the Lady of her fine Riding-Habit, no longer ago than Yesterday, in the Back-lane here? Can you deny that you wished to have her alone in a Wood to strip her, to strip one of the prettiest Ladies that ever was seen in the World? and here you have fallen upon me, and have almost murdered me for doing no Harm to a Girl as willing as myself, only because she likes me better than you.' (XII, viii; 649)

This exposes the personal hypocrisy and immorality of the Master, and implicitly connects these with his artistic failure. By removing 'such low Stuff' (639) as Punch and Joan, the Master has drained all the life out of his puppet-show, and has to rely on the Merry-Andrew to make it pay. People must be amused, as Sleary says to Gradgrind in *Hard Times*, they cannot be always learning.¹³ When the Master sees Sophia he wants, like Blifil, to plunder her materially and sexually, and is hindered by the Merry-Andrew, as Blifil was hindered by Tom. Lacking the true regard for virtue of Tom and the Merry-Andrew, the Master can only present false pretences of it on his stage. These fail to entertain as his sexual ambitions fail because both lack the honest human feeling which would draw the responses they seek. In 'doing no Harm' to a girl as willing as he is, while defending Sophia from attack, the Merry-Andrew enacts the sexual morality which, as we have seen, though not ideal, is clearly superior to the selfish and exploitative behaviour of the villains of the book.

The sequence is interesting for the light it sheds on Fielding's notions of the relationship between art and morality. Professedly moral art, like professedly moral people or behaviour, he immediately suspects of hypocrisy. His response to Richardson's *Pamela* was typical: it was not so much the concept that virtue is rewarded that Fielding objected to as the public profession that virtue would be rewarded tangibly in the here and now. *Tom Jones* can recommend 'the Cause of Religion and Virtue' (7) effectively because it first entertains its readers with an engagingly human story of a tried and proven kind, like the antics of Punch and Joan, and not such modern trumpery as Colley Cibber's part of *The Provok'd Husband*, or *Pamela*, both of which Fielding judged to be more likely to provoke maids like Grace and Pamela to misbehave, and to 'look out after their masters', than to promote true virtue.¹⁴ The accusations of 'lowness' directed at Fielding's writing throughout his career doubtless led him to articulate his defence of his own practice, as opposed to that of self-proclaimedly high-minded and morally-improving writers which he found to be both unentertaining and more likely to debauch than to improve the morals of its audience, and he presents this defence succinctly and dramatically in the puppet-show sequence. The antics of the Merry-Andrew, and of Punch and Joan, may seem more diverting than edifying, but they are proven entertainers, and without genuine entertainment,

---

¹³ David Craig (ed.), Harmondsworth 1969, p. 82.
¹⁴ Martin C. Battestin (ed.), *Joseph Andrews and Shamela*, Boston 1961, p. 338. Colley Cibber, the Poet Laureate, was a frequent target for Fielding's satire. He was the main author of the 'fine and serious' part of *The Provok'd Husband*, the remainder of which was by Vanbrugh. See Charles B. Woods, 'Cibber in Fielding's *Author's Farce*: Three Notes', *Philological Quarterly*, Vol. 44, 1965, pp. 149–51.

there will be no opportunity to edify the spectators. Entertainment which is illuminated by truth to human nature, which both the Master and the author of *Tom Jones* claim, but which the Master fails to achieve in art as in life, is genuine art. It fulfils Horace's injunction to amuse and to instruct and it does so 'without the aid of evangelical puffing and blowing'.[15]

Finally, the puppet sequence differs from the gypsy sequence in that Tom is active and vocal in the former and is supported by the author not with commentary endorsing his opinions but with narrative action which illustrates and extends them. In the latter, Tom is little more than an interested observer, and the authorial commentary carries the burden of the meaning. Tom is a sound judge of entertainment, and a true sounding-board for moral behaviour, but he is not a political theorist. While he carries the reader's affections throughout the narrative, he does not articulate the author's ideas as comprehensively as the commentary. In *Tom Jones*, action and discursive thought complement one another, and the resulting variety is one of the real contrasts defended, albeit light-heartedly and jokingly, in the introductory chapter of Book Five.

An important vehicle for discursive thought in the middle section of *Tom Jones* is again the introductory chapters, which continue to define the nature of Fielding's fiction and the author-reader relationship upon which it is based. It is no accident that the two introductory chapters situated at the centre of the work, those to Books Nine and Ten, define respectively who may write and who should read such fiction. The definitions are enlarged in the neighbouring introductory chapters, which are all concerned in one way or another with the roles of writing and reading. The first chapter of Book Eight, for example, is concerned, as we have seen, with the author's need to balance the factual, which is mundane but convincing, with the marvellous, which is amusing but incredible. In the first chapter of Book Nine we have the definitive account of the Fielding author. It opens with a further reason for the inclusion of introductory essays, which distinguish: 'what is true and genuine in this historic Kind of Writing, from what is false and counterfeit' (IX, i; 487). The author expects his new form to be imitated and he suspects that most of the imitators will be 'incapable of any Degree of Reflection' (488), and will consequently be unable to write introductory essays. These will thus become, by their very presence or absence, a touchstone of the works in question.

[15] Kingsley Amis, *I Like it Here*, London 1961, p. 200.

The author goes on to lament the profusion of romances and novels and the lack of talent of most of their authors:

> To invent good Stories, and to tell them well, are possibly very rare Talents, and yet I have observed few Persons who have scrupled to aim at both. (488)

The most basic, the most essential qualities of the true writer of fiction are thus succinctly stated. The few who possess these talents are, however, almost lost in the mass of would-be romancers and novelists who think paper and ink the only requirements for writing fiction. The author wants to separate *Tom Jones* from the work of such idle and untalented scribblers, and this leads him to reject the term romance, 'a Name with which we might otherwise have been well enough contented' (489), and to insist on calling his work a history. Fielding's debt to the romance has been less fully documented than his debt to the epic: it has been obscured by 'realist' novel criticism claiming Fielding as a pioneer of the new genre, and by his own disparaging references to romances in *Tom Jones*; but the debt is significant, as Henry Knight Miller has recently shown, and as the quoted passage (489) acknowledges.[16] The self-consciously artificial elements of *Tom Jones*, the delight in patterned structure, mythic form, providential plot, stylized character, and highly-wrought style, which are central to the authorial manner of the book, all derive from pre-realist fiction.

With the ground thus cleared of would-be storytellers and their work, the author proceeds with his definition of the qualifications needed to write 'historical' fiction. The first is genius, defined as:

> those Powers of the Mind, which are capable of penetrating into all Things within our Reach and Knowledge, and of distinguishing their essential Differences. These are no other than Invention and Judgment. (490–1)

Invention is then further defined not as 'a creative Faculty', but in its original Latin meaning of 'Discovery, or finding out ... a quick and sagacious Penetration into the true Essence of all the Objects of our Contemplation' (491). Invention and judgement are, in fact, virtually the

---

[16] See *Henry Fielding's 'Tom Jones' and the Romance Tradition*; and Sheridan Baker, 'Henry Fielding's Comic Romances', *Papers of the Michigan Academy of Science, Arts, and Letters*, Vol. XLV, 1960, pp. 411–19.

same; and both, essentially, are equivalent to penetration. This definition of genius gives a very useful insight into the purpose of *Tom Jones*. In the Dedication to Lyttleton, Fielding suggested that: 'it is much easier to make good Men wise, than to make bad Men good' (8); and in his 'Essay on the Knowledge of the Characters of Men' he repeatedly urged the need to alert the good to the practices of the bad, which they can thwart if only they can anticipate them. Penetration, the kind of suspicion that Sophia has and Tom has not, and must learn if he is to survive, is the key defence of the good against the bad. Those who have it, have a duty to put it at the service of those who have not. Sophia will guide Tom, whose natural talents have drawn him to aspire after wisdom, and to ally himself to it. The author possessed of genius will similarly offer guidance to the reader whose natural talents lead him to seek to forestall evil by penetrating its devices. It follows that an author who sets up as a guide in penetration must himself be especially qualified in that field, and this is a point made repeatedly in *Tom Jones*: 'no Author ought to write any Thing besides Dictionaries and Spelling-Books who hath not this Privilege', that is, who is not: 'admitted behind the Scenes of this great Theatre of Nature' (VII, i; 327). For Fielding, art which does not send us back to life better informed than we were, is at best mere entertainment and a waste of time. An author worthy to belong to his 'Order of Historians' will have a special insight into the workings of human nature to communicate to his reader.

The other qualities such an author needs are learning, conversation 'with all Ranks and Degrees of Men', and 'a good Heart' (494). Learning is necessary, it is argued, if the talents supplied by nature are to be put to effective use. The idea is a Renaissance one, which even in Fielding's time was losing support. The learned Dr Johnson preferred the novels of his unlearned friend Richardson to those of Fielding. The novels of Defoe, ignored by the contemporary literary establishment, have always been popular, and have long been critically respectable. Dickens' lack of learning did not prevent him becoming one of the greatest of English novelists. The evidence of history is against Fielding's view. 'Conversation' or familiarity with all levels of society will be more readily conceded as a necessary qualification for a writer, particularly one who takes a panoramic view of society. The final qualification, the possession of 'a good Heart', has proved the most contentious. It is defined, with reference to Horace, as the capacity to feel the emotions that are to be portrayed:

> no Man can paint a Distress well, which he doth not feel while he is painting it . . . In the same Manner . . . I am convinced I never make

my Reader laugh heartily, but where I have laughed before him. (494)[17]

Frank Kermode, who is scathing about the 'Good Heart' as 'an adequate criterion for moral judgment', does not perceive how far the concept of good nature extends in Fielding's thought.[18] In *The Champion* he defines it as:

> a delight in the happiness of mankind, and a concern at their misery, with a desire, as much as possible, to procure the former, and avert the latter; and this, with a constant regard to desert.[19]

He argues that it 'gilds over all our other virtues' and enables us 'to pass through all the offices and stations of life with real merit'. Indeed it draws us near to 'the benevolent Creator' who is 'the best-natured being in the universe'.[20] Tom, we are later told, in the author's best ironic manner:

> was one of the best-natured Fellows alive, and had all that Weakness which is called Compassion, and which distinguishes this imperfect Character from that noble Firmness of Mind, which rolls a Man, as it were, within himself, and, like a polished Bowl, enables him to run through the World without being once stopped by the Calamities which happen to others. (XIV, vi; 760–1)

This capacity for imaginative sympathy with other people is both a moral and an artistic virtue, and the ability to create sympathetic feelings in one's readers is, according to Horace and Pope, what makes a poet a poet:

> ... He, who gives my breast a thousand pains,
> Can make me feel each Passion that he feigns,
> Inrage, compose, with more than magic Art,
> With Pity, and with Terror, tear my heart;

---

[17] Perhaps the severest comment is Sir John Hawkins': 'He was the inventor of that cant-phrase, goodness of heart, which is every day used as a substitute for probity, and means little more than the virtue of a horse or a dog'. Paulson and Lockwood (eds), *Henry Fielding: The Critical Heritage*, p. 446.
[18] 'Richardson and Fielding', *Cambridge Journal*, Vol. IV, 1950, p. 109.
[19] Henley, Vol. XV, p. 258. Cf. Miller (ed.), *Miscellanies by Henry Fielding, Esq; Volume One*, p. 158.
[20] Henley, Vol. XV, pp. 259–60.

> And snatch me, o'er the earth, or thro' the air,
> To Thebes, to Athens, when he will, and where.[21]

The author of *Tom Jones* feels this sympathy for those of his characters, like Tom, who feel it for others, and who act accordingly, but he does not extend it to self-contained villains like Blifil. And within the world of the book, it is not extended by the good to the bad, nor by the bad to the good. Fielding's villains invariably think his good men are fools; and they usually overreach themselves because of this misunderstanding. Fielding's good men fail to anticipate and to ward off the depredations of the bad, because they misunderstand, and fail to empathize with the machinations of such black hearts. One only has to think of the very real bond of understanding between Richardson's saintly Clarissa and the villainous Lovelace to remind oneself that this need not be so. Blifil is a singularly unrealized villain when compared to Lovelace, say, or Milton's Satan, and while Fielding might respond that in being evil he is essentially devoid of animating humanity, this does not explain the imbalance of empathy with the good and bad characters. No one has puzzled over Blifil as over Iago or Satan: like Milton's God he can be defended as a theoretical concept, but not responded to as a human figure. If Milton makes his devil too human, Fielding makes his villain too distant from the reader's sympathy. It is the prevalence of evil that maintains the ultimate balance in *Tom Jones*, not its embodiment in a single menacing figure.

In the introductory chapter to Book Ten the author turns from describing himself to describing his reader. The placing of this chapter immediately after the centre of the book, in a complementary position to the definition of the qualifications of an author in Book Nine Chapter One, is one of the many symmetries, small and large, which revolve about this central point. The great difference between author and reader—that the author is a single, known person while the reader is multiple, diverse, and unknown—is immediately and wittily acknowledged in a passage we have already looked at briefly:

> Reader, it is impossible we should know what Sort of Person thou wilt be: For, perhaps, thou may'st be as learned in Human Nature as *Shakespear* himself was, and, perhaps, thou may'st be no wiser than some of his Editors. (X, i; 523)

The effect of this frank admission that readers vary widely is to interrupt the one-to-one illusion that much novel reading is based upon, and to

---

[21] *The First Epistle of the Second Book of Horace Imitated: To Augustus*, ll. 342–7. Butt (ed.), *The Poems of Alexander Pope*, p. 647.

prompt the actual reader to look to his reading talents. The simple ability to read is no more an adequate qualification for reading *Tom Jones* than the possession of paper, pen and ink is for writing it. The qualifications for reading which the author goes on to list are suggestive rather than inclusive, in keeping with his practice of interspersing numerous, succinct, and mutually interdependent passages of fictional theory throughout the narrative. They are, however, essential to a correct reading of *Tom Jones*.

The first qualification insisted upon is the willingness of the reader to suspend judgement on the part until it can be seen in terms of the whole:

> for a little Reptile of a Critic to presume to find Fault with any of its Parts, without knowing the Manner in which the Whole is connected, and before he comes to the final Catastrophe, is a most presumptuous Absurdity. (525)

Behind the playfully exaggerated hostility of this comment, drawn no doubt from Fielding's youthful experience of seeing plays, including his own, vociferously condemned before they could be completed, is the serious point that the created world of *Tom Jones*, like the larger world created by God, which it imitates and reflects, can only properly be understood when seen as a whole to which all the parts contribute. The religious belief that, as Pope expressed it, 'Whatever is, is Right', has long been out of favour, but it was meaningful for Fielding.[22] It was not only his plot that was painstakingly planned. The moral pattern of the book can only be recovered by a reader willing to hold in his mind and amalgamate all the actions of a particular character and all of the comments on those actions by other characters and by the author, together with the complementary actions and comments upon those actions, of other characters, before he makes a final moral judgement upon that character. The process needs to be repeated for each of the important characters, and the resulting assessments must then be pieced together to form the total pattern. The modern practice of reading by the seat of one's pants, and not pausing for reflection until the work is completed, is not appropriate to *Tom Jones* because, as this passage makes clear, it was not written for that sort of reading.

Discernment and learning were defined in the previous introductory chapter as the other essential qualifications for the Fielding author, and it is no surprise to find that the Fielding reader is expected to match those talents. Finally in this chapter the reader is admonished:

---

[22] *An Essay on Man*, I, 294. *Poems*, p. 515.

> not to condemn a Character as a bad one, because it is not perfectly a
> good one. If thou dost delight in these Models of Perfection, there are
> Books enow written to gratify thy Taste; but as we have not, in the
> Course of our Conversation, ever happened to meet with any such
> Person, we have not chosen to introduce any such here. (526)

This briefly restates three crucial points made earlier about the art of *Tom Jones*. It is human nature, and not a literary apotheosis of it, that is the subject of the book. Knowledge of human nature, which can only be acquired from a wide-ranging conversation with all degrees of people, teaches that it is almost invariably mixed, that the good are almost always flawed and the bad have almost always some redeeming features. The way, therefore, to influence the reader for the better is to create such mixed characters, thus ensuring that:

> The Foibles and Vices of Men in whom there is great Mixture of Good,
> become more glaring Objects, from the Virtues which contrast them,
> and shew their Deformity; and when we find such Vices attended with
> their evil Consequence to our favourite Characters, we are not only
> taught to shun them for our own Sake, but to hate them for the
> Mischiefs they have already brought on those we love. (527)

If Tom's sexual and other misdemeanours, and Allworthy's failures of judgement had consistently been read in the light of this comment a good deal of facile commentary on Fielding's supposedly deficient morality might not have emerged to obscure what really happens in *Tom Jones*.

Before we leave the central six books there is a crucial statement about the doctrine of *Tom Jones* that needs to be considered. At the conclusion of the puppet-show affair Tom and Partridge again set out in pursuit of Sophia. A storm sends them into an inn, where they chance upon the boy who rode before her. Tom questions the boy in private, 'for so delicate was he with regard to *Sophia*, that he never willingly mentioned her Name in the Presence of many People' (XII, viii; 651). The author observes that it was ironic, in view of this delicacy, that Tom's separation from Sophia since Upton was due:

> to the supposed Want of that Delicacy with which he so abounded; for
> in reality *Sophia* was much more offended at the Freedoms which she
> thought, and not without good Reason, he had taken with her Name
> and Character, than at any Freedoms, in which, under his present
> Circumstances, he had indulged himself with the Person of another
> Woman. (651)

Then follows one of the most interesting comments on the moral significance of *Tom Jones* as a whole, which begins with the particular matter to hand, but goes on to expand to the most general doctrinal content of the work:

> But so Matters fell out, and so I must relate them; and if any Reader is shocked at their appearing unnatural, I cannot help it. I must remind such Persons, that I am not writing a System, but a History, and I am not obliged to reconcile every Matter to the received Notions concerning Truth and Nature. But if this was never so easy to do, perhaps it might be more prudent in me to avoid it. For Instance, as the Fact at present before us now stands, without any Comment of mine upon it, tho' it may at first Sight offend some Readers, yet upon more mature Consideration, it must please all; for wise and good Men may consider what happened to *Jones* at *Upton* as a just Punishment for his Wickedness, with Regard to Women, of which it was indeed the immediate Consequence; and silly and bad persons may comfort themselves in their Vices, by flattering their own Hearts that the Characters of Men are rather owing to Accident than to Virtue. Now perhaps the Reflections which we should be here inclined to draw, would alike contradict both these Conclusions, and would shew that these Incidents contribute only to confirm the great, useful and uncommon Doctrine, which it is the Purpose of this whole Work to inculcate, and which we must not fill up our Pages by frequently repeating, as an ordinary Parson fills his Sermon by repeating his Text at the End of every Paragraph. (651–2)

William Empson calls the technique employed here 'double irony'.[23] The author offers two interpretations of what happened, assigning one to 'wise and good Men', and one to 'silly and bad persons', and then dissociates himself from both. He declines to state his own judgement, but suggests that if the reader can work it out, he will have found 'the great, useful and uncommon Doctrine, which it is the Purpose of this whole Work to inculcate'. This challenge to the reader to go beyond the stereotyped interpretations cited is a revealing indication of how the author would like all the book to be read, at least by the 'upper Graduates in Criticism' (III, i; 117).

Taking up the challenge, we may proceed through the rejected alternatives in pursuit of the doctrine. Those readers who deduce that 'the Characters of Men are rather owing to Accident than to Virtue' are silly because they omit prudence and moral effort from their view of character,

---

[23] 'Tom Jones' in Paulson (ed.), *Fielding: A Collection of Critical Essays*, p. 126.

and bad because they thereby encourage the view that virtue is accidental, and no credit to its possessor. While it is clear that *Tom Jones* refutes such a doctrine, it must also be admitted that Tom's good nature owes much to the accidents of his birth and upbringing. Fielding had no clearer solution to the nature/nurture debate than anyone else. He was not a determinist, but he recognized that chance, genetic and otherwise, played a significant role in human affairs. So we have a double irony even in this first, most readily rejected interpretation. The 'wise and good Men' who adopt the second interpretation, that 'what happened to *Jones* at *Upton*' was 'a just Punishment for his Wickedness, with Regard to Women', are a little over-subtle in their interpretation of the workings of providence. A wise man might more sanguinely expect this sort of poetic justice to occur in art than in life. Ironically enough, *Tom Jones* does conclude with a scrupulous administration of poetic justice, as the author half anticipates when he adds that Tom's punishment 'was the immediate Consequence' of his lapse with Mrs Waters. The wise and good readers are also a little over-righteous in their condemnation of this lapse. We have just been told that Sophia, the best judge in the book, and the one most personally concerned, was a good deal less offended with the sexual escapade than with the supposedly free use made of her name in disreputable quarters. We have also seen that the author, while in no sense excusing Tom's fault, went out of his way to extenuate the circumstances and the consequent guilt. Fielding put his view succinctly in *The Crisis: A Sermon* (1741), when he said of fornication: 'a great and abominable Sin, no Doubt it is: Yet such as would hardly bring down the Judgment of God on a whole People'.[24] The truly wise reader then will be less hasty to condemn than the 'wise and good Men', and less ready to expect punishments to follow hard upon crimes, even in a fictional context in which the author plays God.

But even he will not find it easy to deduce what conclusions the author would be inclined to draw, which would contradict both these responses. There is ambiguity, and double irony, surrounding both postulated interpretations, so much so, indeed, that the total irony must be called multiple and many-layered. If there is a great doctrine to be found in the midst of all this judicious balancing of alternatives, as the author avers, then I would suggest that it is that virtue is, and must be, its own reward, since it is seldom rewarded on this side of the grave. Virtue is as Fielding said in the Dedication (7) the only way a man may live at peace with himself, whatever other rewards it may bring. And if happiness is to be

[24] London 1741, p. 2.

found on earth, it can only be found by the virtuous: virtue is a sufficient condition for peace of mind, and a necessary, though not always a sufficient condition for happiness.

Coleridge remarked perceptively that Fielding distinguishes between what a man is, and what he does:

> If I want a servant or mechanic, I wish to know what he does:—but of a friend, I must know what he is. And in no writer is this momentous distinction so finely brought forward as by Fielding.[25]

It must be added that Fielding is also one of the most expert of novelists in exposing the differences between what characters say and what they do, and in insisting on the latter as the sure guide to what they are. This test is applied, typically, to the hypocrites who people the book. The good characters, like Tom, who are not hypocrites, fall into the other category described by Coleridge, and the author's own position in the passage quoted is, I think, that rewards and punishments are ultimately irrelevant to the essentially good man, like Tom, who:

> had Somewhat about him ... whose Use is not so properly to distinguish Right from Wrong, as to prompt and incite [him] to the former, and to restrain and with-hold [him] from the latter ... though he did not always act rightly, yet he never did otherwise without feeling and suffering for it. (IV, vi; 171–3)

Tom demonstrates the effect of this quality by deciding to quit Sophia lest he harm her. He too is to be judged by his actions, good or faulty, but his essential virtue is defined in this passage, and it is for that that we love him, and wish him happy.

The effect of the author's long comment on the doctrine of his work is, in a final irony, not to simplify the interpretation of the reader, but to render it more complex and sophisticated. No reader who relies on being told, instead of deducing for himself, what the doctrine is, can hope to understand the novel fully. This is the real separation of the book's readers which stands behind the many rhetorical separations of the postulated readers into such classes as 'wise and good' and 'silly and bad'. There are more Blifils and Dowlings in the world of the novel than there are Sophias, and the author expects no better of the audience who will read it, an expectation borne out by the history of *Tom Jones* criticism. For every Coleridge, who perceived the book's celebration of virtue, there

---

[25] Blanchard, *Fielding the Novelist*, p. 320.

have been more than enough readers who found it 'corrupting', like Sir John Hawkins; vacuous, like F. R. Leavis; or harmlessly libertine, like W. Somerset Maugham.[26] The reader who gives due consideration to the author's comments at this point will not find it easy to join in these dismissals. Throughout *Tom Jones* the commentary, so often ignored or skipped over, transforms the meaning of the narrative.[27] Its addition is chemical not mathematical. Narrative and commentary interact to produce a compound more complex than the sum of its ingredients. Incidents and characters are distanced, and placed in a framework of artifice, which makes them at once natural and comic, moving and yet puppets, the concern and the delight of the reader. The author has a complex role in this process, as Henry Knight Miller observes:

> Intimately and personally engaged on the great comic battleground of human nature he was: but he also sat on a high seat above it, a benignant umpire, and afforded each side its due.[28]

The reader whose qualifications are sufficient is invited to join the author in this multi-levelled engagement with the fictional world of *Tom Jones*. The discussion of Tom's 'punishment' after Upton is only the most overt of many such invitations in the book. Its placement near the end of the second six-book segment is significant. It indicates the author's belief that the reader has read enough of the work to be able to make an educated guess at its 'great, useful and uncommon Doctrine', and to take that guess with him into the final third of the book, where he can test it against the ultimate experiences of Tom, Sophia and Allworthy, and so reach a final conclusion about its nature and worth.

---

[26] See Paulson and Lockwood (eds), *Fielding: The Critical Heritage*, p. 446; F. R. Leavis, *The Great Tradition*, London 1948, pp. 3–4; and W. Somerset Maugham, 'Henry Fielding and *Tom Jones*' in *Ten Novels and Their Authors*, London 1954, p. 41.

[27] Even so perceptive a critic as William Empson describes Book Nine Chapter One as a 'chapter of introductory prattle'. 'Tom Jones', p. 144.

[28] *Essays on Fielding's Miscellanies*, p. 269.

Chapter Three

The last third of *Tom Jones* opens with an invocation. The placing of this invocation here is no mere whimsy, like the placing of the Author's Preface in the middle of the third volume of *Tristram Shandy*. In the last six books Tom experiences both the low and high extremes of his fortunes and he comes to terms with the lessons of prudence and virtue. The doctrine of the book is ultimately worked out, and the complicated plot is brought to a triumphant conclusion. Before undertaking these considerable tasks the author may well have felt in need of inspiration, and he paused, briefly, to remind himself and his reader of the heights to which he aspired, and of the standards by which he wanted *Tom Jones* to be judged. In typical manner his invocation yokes together the 'bright Love of Fame' and that 'much plumper Dame' the need for money. He looks forward both to being read 'with Honour', and to making money to support: 'the prattling Babes, whose innocent Play hath often been interrupted by my Labours' (XIII, i; 683-5). His ambitions are proclaimed in the first paragraph, which calls upon the epic muse, Calliope, who inspired Homer, Virgil, and Milton; but the author quickly turns from the traditional to the personal:

> Foretel me that some tender Maid, whose Grandmother is yet unborn, hereafter, when, under the fictitious Name of *Sophia*, she reads the real Worth which once existed in my *Charlotte*, shall, from her sympathetic Breast, send forth the heaving Sigh... Comfort me by a solemn Assurance, that when the little Parlour in which I sit at this Instant, shall be reduced to a worse furnished Box, I shall be read, with Honour, by those who never knew nor saw me, and whom I shall neither know nor see. (683)

The epic invocation is thus incorporated into the new species of fiction, which is less sublime and more comic, less heroic and more domestic, less public and more personal, less elevated and more satiric and picaresque. After the three great epic poets the author invokes the spirit of Aristophanes, Lucian, Cervantes, Rabelais, Molière, Shakespeare, Swift and Marivaux, all great comic writers whose work defines the tradition to which *Tom Jones* belongs.

The narrative opens with Tom in London, seeking out the house of the Irish peer who has befriended Mrs Fitzpatrick, so that he can return Sophia's pocketbook with its £100 note enclosed. London is to be the scene of the final third of the book. It is a grim, urban wasteland of hypocrisy, deceit, oppression and exploitation. In Book Seventeen, for example, the author comments on the hunting of women and money that takes place in the city:

> I have often considered a very fine young Woman of Fortune and Fashion, when first found strayed from the Pale of her Nursery, to be in pretty much the same Situation [as a doe who strays from the forest, and is hunted by villager and squire] . . . The Town is immediately in an Uproar, she is hunted from Park to Play, from Court to Assembly, from Assembly to her own Chamber, and rarely escapes a single Season from the Jaws of some Devourer or other: For if her Friends protect her from some, it is only to deliver her over to one of their own chusing, often more disagreeable to her than any of the rest. (XVII, iv; 887)

The hunting image is appropriate not only because Sophia is the daughter of the fox-hunting Western but also because she is treated like a carcass to be sold to the highest bidder, and those who pursue her are interested only in the quality of the carcass and the dead weight of the accompanying money. Such persecution is not, of course, limited to the city of London. Western, who despises the city and all its ways, is relentless in his determination that she shall marry the man of his choice. But when the author comments on the brutality of this parental bullying he chooses images from London to express his intense distaste for the marrying of girls like animals:

> *Western* beheld the deplorable Condition of his Daughter with no more Contrition or Remorse, than the Turnkey of *Newgate* feels at viewing the Agonies of a tender Wife, when taking her last Farewel of her condemned Husband; or rather he looked down on her with the same Emotions which arise in an honest fair Tradesman, who sees his Debtor dragged to Prison for 10 *l.* which, though a just Debt, the Wretch is wickedly unable to pay. Or, to hit the Case still more nearly, he felt the

same Compunction with a Bawd when some poor Innocent whom she hath ensnared into her Hands, falls into Fits at the first Proposal of what is called seeing Company. Indeed this Resemblance would be exact, was it not that the Bawd hath an Interest in what she doth, and the Father, though perhaps he may blindly think otherwise, can in Reality have none in urging his Daughter to almost an equal Prostitution. (XVI, ii; 840)

The prison and bawdy-house images, with their unmistakably urban colouring, shape the author's rhetoric as he zeroes remorselessly in on the final word 'prostitution' to describe forced marriages. In London Sophia is pursued, hawked about by her relatives, abused, imprisoned, and almost raped; the last at the suggestion and with the connivance of her aunt's cousin, Lady Bellaston. If the country is Paradise in *Tom Jones* then the city is Hell, and if Blifil is the serpent in Paradise, Lady Bellaston is a she-devil in that Hell. She first seduces and then persecutes Tom; she separates Tom and Sophia; and she persecutes Sophia. She very nearly succeeds in her schemes to have Tom press-ganged and Sophia raped. And she is an altogether more human and therefore more threatening figure of evil than Blifil ever becomes. We see her persuading Lord Fellamar to rape Sophia:

> 'You force me to use a strange Kind of Language, and to betray my Sex most abominably: But I am contented with knowing my Intentions are good, and that I am endeavouring to serve my Cousin; for I think you will make her a Husband notwithstanding this; or, upon my Soul, I would not even persuade her to fling herself away upon an empty Title. She should not upbraid me hereafter with having lost a Man of Spirit; for that his Enemies allow this poor young Fellow to be.'
>
> Let those who have had the Satisfaction of hearing Reflections of this Kind from a Wife or a Mistress, declare whether they are at all sweetened by coming from a Female Tongue. Certain it is they sunk deeper into his Lordship, than any Thing which *Demosthenes* or *Cicero* could have said on the Occasion.
>
> Lady *Bellaston* perceiving she had fired the young Lord's Pride, began now, like a true Orator, to rouse other Passions to its Assistance. (XV, iv; 795)

We never see Blifil work other people to his purposes with such skill. Lady Bellaston is an altogether more sophisticated figure of evil than any of the other villains in the book. She combines the malevolent rhetoric of Milton's Satan with the unerring aim of Lady Macbeth. As a result the London sequence, over which she presides, is more menacing than Blifil's plotting in the first six books or the dangers posed by the assorted ruffians of the central, picaresque section. She is more credible than Blifil partly because she is better motivated. The author's comment on her persisting with the match between Sophia and Fellamar after the rape has failed is an example:

> But perhaps the Reader may wonder why Lady *Bellaston*, who in her Heart hated *Sophia*, should be so desirous of promoting a Match, which was so much in the Interest of the young Lady. Now I would desire such Readers to look carefully into human Nature, Page almost the last, and there he will find . . . that a Woman who hath once been pleased with the Possession of a Man, will go above half way to the Devil, to prevent any other Woman from enjoying the same. (XVI, viii; 866)

The ease with which Lady Bellaston seduces Tom and induces him to accept payment for his services has troubled even staunch supporters of *Tom Jones* like Coleridge.[1] It happens almost as soon as Tom sets foot in London and it demonstrates how ill-equipped he is to match the accomplishment of a Lady Bellaston. His third sexual entanglement is certainly the most unsavoury, and his seduction the most perfunctory. In place of the elaborate explanations and defences of Tom's two earlier lapses is the blunt statement:

> *Jones* had never less Inclination to an Amour than at present; but Gallantry to the Ladies was among his Principles of Honour; and he held it as much incumbent on him to accept a Challenge to Love, as if it had been a Challenge to Fight. Nay, his very Love to *Sophia* made it necessary for him to keep well with the Lady, as he made no doubt but she was capable of bringing him into the Presence of the other. (XIII, vii; 715)

Two chapters later there is a defence of Tom's unfashionable honouring of his contract with Lady Bellaston:

> He knew the tacit Consideration upon which all her Favours were conferred; and as his Necessity obliged him to accept them, so his Honour, he concluded, forced him to pay the Price. (XIII, ix; 724)

In neither context, however, is it suggested that Tom's appetite is aroused, as it had been with Molly and Mrs Waters, and his initial

---

[1] Coleridge called it the 'most questionable part of *Tom Jones*'. See Blanchard, *Fielding the Novelist*, p. 319.

acceptance of Lady Bellaston's favours remains calculated. Tom acts on principle, and from self-interest; there is no passion. We have already seen in the Northerton episode that his principle of honour about challenges to fight is mistaken. In London Tom is to fight again, when challenged by Fitzpatrick, and to learn that even the knowledge that he fought in self-defence is poor consolation when he thinks he has killed a man. Since the author makes the comparison between the two challenges to 'honour', the reader may be sure that Tom's principle of gallantry is also mistaken. Tom's pursuit of self-interest is as inept as his 'Principles of Honour' are false. He thinks he is talking to Mrs Fitzpatrick, not Lady Bellaston, and though the latter can, in fact, lead him to Sophia as surely as the former, the worst possible way to enlist the lady's support in finding Sophia is to begin an affair with her and so give her the strongest of motives to keep them apart. The facts that the lady is masked and the affair is begun at a Masquerade, reflect the deceptions the London world will practise on a raw recruit. Fielding detested Masquerades, as *Amelia* in particular makes apparent, and his choice of one as the scene for Tom's most serious error is characteristic.² The masks, which image hypocrisy, do not deceive the regular patrons, as the lady informs Tom:

> You cannot conceive any Thing more insipid and childish than a Masquerade to the People of Fashion, who in general know one another as well here, as when they meet in an Assembly or a Drawing-room. (716)

But they cloud the perceptions of an innocent like Tom, who is never more wrong than when he accepts Lady Bellaston's challenge.

Book Thirteen sees the beginning not only of Tom's least glorious entanglement but also of the two counterplots which ultimately extricate him from his difficulties. Despite the best-laid plans of Lady Bellaston, Tom and Sophia meet accidentally at her house, and Tom has the opportunity to ask pardon for what happened at Upton and, more importantly, to remove Sophia's mistaken resentment at his supposedly free use of her name. It was this latter which prompted the author's reflection on his 'great, useful and uncommon Doctrine' in the previous Book. In view of his refusal to comment then on his own assessment of the matter, it is interesting to see him arranging for the misunderstanding

---

² See *Amelia*, VII, vi–vii; X, ii–iv. Fielding's first published work was a poem, *The Masquerade* (1728). Cf. *Miscellanies*, p. 155; and Maurice Johnson, 'The Sermon at the Masquerade' in *Fielding's Art of Fiction*, Philadelphia 1961, pp. 157–64.

which had alienated the affections of Sophia to be so promptly removed. Truth will out, clearly, and that is one of the great weapons vindicating the virtuous and exposing the vicious. Tom, however, is by no means vindicated yet, for he is asking pardon for one sexual betrayal of Sophia while embarked upon another, and in circumstances which virtually ensure that the truth about it will out as well, and before very long. It is therefore not surprising that his speech lacks ease, though his sentiments are unexceptionable. Tom and Sophia are never witty lovers like Beatrice and Benedick or Mirabel and Millamant, and this scene is no exception. But they do meet for the first time since Somerset and they do come to a better understanding of one another. The external obstacles to their union remain, but their commitment to one another is greatly strengthened.

The second counterplot involves Enderson, the would-be highwayman, the Miller family, and Nightingale. It is a story from which Tom emerges in an entirely creditable way, with his personal morality, so lately impugned, reaffirmed as generous and admirable. He also gains the staunchest of friends and advocates in Mrs Miller, who is largely responsible for setting Tom's record straight with the two people whose opinion of him matters most, Allworthy and Sophia. It is Tom's generosity to Enderson and his family which first predisposes Mrs Miller to feel gratitude towards him. Tom offers her £50, all he has, to relieve their distress. Immediately afterwards, Nightingale offers a guinea if a collection is made, an offer which is verbal, public, and not, in the event, carried through. Tom's action had been substantial, private, and more than generous, and the contrast between the two leads the author to make one of his wry reflections on charity, juxtaposing the self-congratulatory attitude of the givers of charity with the ungrateful response of the receivers (XIII, viii; 722). When Enderson appears to thank Tom in person for preserving his family, Tom realizes that he was the highwayman who tried to rob him near London and whom he released despite Partridge's protests. Tom is again generous in preventing Enderson from betraying this desperate act to his cousin Mrs Miller.[3] When that lady expresses heartfelt gratitude to Tom, he responds with a sentiment that is central to Fielding's thought:

> If there are Men who cannot feel the Delight of giving Happiness to others, I sincerely pity them, as they are incapable of tasting what is, in

---

[3] Partridge later reveals Enderson's secret to Mrs Miller (XIV, iii; 750–1), indicating that truth will out even when it is concealed from generous motives.

my Opinion, a greater Honour, a higher Interest, and a sweeter Pleasure, than the ambitious, the avaritious, or the voluptuous Man can ever obtain. (XIII, x; 728)

Tom has learned his principles of generosity from Allworthy, who makes his benefactions to people like Mrs Miller not simply out of a sense of duty but also for the pleasure it gives him.

Tom is to incur a more personal gratitude from Mrs Miller for his intervention in the Nightingale-Nancy Miller affair. Immediately after one of Lady Bellaston's visits to Tom's room, Mrs Miller asks him to leave the house because of the reflection his entertaining of Lady Bellaston might cast on her reputation and the character of her daughters. Tom does not resent this reproof as another man might, and when Nightingale comes in immediately after and acquaints Tom with his intention of leaving Nancy because his father, who controls his fortune, has provided him with another match, Tom rebukes him for toying with the girl's affections. Nightingale responds by reminding Tom of his last night's visitor, to which Tom replies:

> Lookee, Mr. *Nightingale* . . . I am no canting Hypocrite, nor do I pretend to the Gift of Chastity, more than my Neighbours. I have been guilty with Women, I own it; but am not conscious that I have ever injured any—nor would I to procure Pleasure to myself, be knowingly the Cause of Misery to any human Being. (XIV, iv; 755)

In the decision he has to make Nightingale is torn between worldly wisdom and his real affection for Nancy. Tom can speak so persuasively to him here because his experience with women makes him appear a man of the world and not a prude or a hypocrite. In this way Tom's worst lapse is turned to good account, only one of the ironies in this finely constructed sequence. Tom acts to preserve the peace and happiness of a lady who has just asked him to leave her house because of his immoral example. That immoral example is used to persuade Nightingale to behave morally towards Nancy. And Nancy and Nightingale have already anticipated the marriage ceremony without any prompting from Tom's example, though Mrs Miller does not know it at this point.

Tom, who later intercedes with Nightingale's father and arranges for the marriage to take place before Nightingale can be persuaded by others that it is against his worldly interest, shows a real concern for the happiness of Nancy and Nightingale. The author, while warmly endorsing Tom's disinterested generosity, does not lose sight of the contrary opinion that is widely accepted in society. In typical manner he sets up a dialogue between Tom and Nightingale, in which the contrary opinions are urged:

> But as the World, I know not well for what Reason, agree to see this Treachery [deceiving women] in a better Light, he [Nightingale] was so far from being ashamed of his Iniquities of this Kind, that he gloried in them, and would often boast of his Skill in gaining of Women, and his Triumphs over their Hearts, for which he had before this time received some Rebukes from *Jones*, who always exprest great Bitterness against any Misbehaviour to the fair Part of the Species, who, if considered, he said, as they ought to be, in the Light of the dearest Friends, were to be cultivated, honoured, and caressed with the utmost Love and Tenderness; but if regarded as Enemies, were a Conquest of which a Man ought rather to be ashamed than to value himself upon it. (XIV, iv; 756)

While there is no doubt that the author seconds Tom's sentiments here and rejects the rakish code, he nonetheless allows those who remain convinced that Nightingale has imprudently sacrificed his worldly interest to mere sentimentality to have the last laugh. Nightingale, we are told:

> was now ready drest, and full as sober as many of my Readers will think a Man ought to be who receives a Wife in so imprudent a Manner. (XV, viii; 814)

The author here as elsewhere in the book retreats from close involvement with the narrative to an Olympian detachment, which allows him to laugh at what he also cares deeply about.

Tom's part in the Nightingale episode is summarized by the author in a comment which elaborates and reinforces Tom's own comment on the pleasure helping Enderson gave him. Tom was not, we are told, disinterested or unconcerned in the matter because he was:

> one who could truly say with him in *Terence, Homo sum: Humani nihil a me alienum puto*. He was never an indifferent Spectator of the Misery or Happiness of any one; and he felt either the one or the other in greater Proportion as he himself contributed to either. He could not therefore be the Instrument of raising a whole Family from the lowest State of Wretchedness to the highest Pitch of Joy without conveying great Felicity to himself; more perhaps than worldly Men often purchase to

themselves by undergoing the most severe Labour, and often by wading through the deepest Iniquity. (XV, viii; 815–16)

Tom's reward is not to be confined to such pleasures, since his actions have won him the active and determined gratitude of those involved, particularly Mrs Miller. The latter reward is not as immediate as the former, however, and Tom's own affairs remain in a sorry state while he is effectively furthering those of others. In Book Fifteen the focus shifts away from Tom and his difficulties to the plots of Lady Bellaston against Sophia.

The threatened rape of Sophia by Lord Fellamar is, as we have seen, a diabolical scheme. The author calls it 'the most tragical Matter in our whole History' (XV, iv; 796), and there is no reason to suspect him of irony at this point, though he may be taking a parodic glance at *Clarissa*. The boisterous entrance of Squire Western at the crucial moment certainly tumbles the scene back into comedy, but the threat, so luckily averted, remains as part of the sinister backdrop of London, and indeed of evil throughout the book. If the three central characters are surrounded by a sunny halo of comic providence, the dark background is forever threatening to engulf them. There is a real tension between the dark, Hogarthian vision of the bulk of human life, and the bright play of the spotlight on Tom, Sophia, and Allworthy throughout *Tom Jones*. The fact that the evil is thwarted by the author's providential control does not suggest that he believes divine providence will act similarly in real life; indeed he specifically rejects such a view in the first sentence of this Book:

> There are a Set of Religious, or rather Moral Writers, who teach that Virtue is the certain Road to Happiness, and Vice to Misery in this World. A very wholsome and comfortable Doctrine, and to which we have but one Objection, namely, That it is not true. (XV, i; 783)

In the discussion which follows the author distinguishes between two kinds of virtue. 'The Exercise of those Cardinal Virtues, which like good House-wives stay at home, and mind only the Business of their own Family' is one kind of virtue which does lead to happiness in this life, and which should rather be called 'Wisdom', though in a limited sense of that term. The other kind of virtue is:

> a certain relative Quality, which is always busying itself without Doors, and seems as much interested in pursuing the Good of others as its own. (783)

Not only is this not productive of human happiness to its practitioner, it leads to 'Poverty and Contempt, with all the Mischiefs which Backbiting, Envy, and Ingratitude can bring on Mankind in our Idea of Happiness' (784). This theoretical distinction is then applied to the narrative:

> while Mr. *Jones* was acting the most virtuous Part imaginable in labouring to preserve his fellow Creatures from Destruction, the Devil, or some other evil Spirit, one perhaps cloathed in human Flesh, was hard at Work to make him completely miserable in the Ruin of his *Sophia*. (784)

This makes it clear that the author regards his second definition of virtue as the truer one. Like Milton, he cannot praise a fugitive and cloistered virtue, preferring one which sallies forth actively into the world and involves itself with the good of others. While the exercise of this virtue brings Tom a pleasure impervious to the contempt and envy of the world, it is unlikely to procure his happiness, and this is 'one of the noblest Arguments that Reason alone can furnish for the Belief of Immortality'. Providence will ultimately reward such virtue appropriately, but it may not be until a future life. In the novel, however, the author can have it both ways. He makes it clear that Tom comes within an ace of misery and that that result would follow naturally from the action in which he involves himself; but he also uses his own providential power to arrange the rescue of Tom and to make him 'the happiest of all human Kind' (XVIII, xiii; 979). If life does not always imitate art in rewarding the virtuous, virtue remains a compellingly attractive alternative to the hermitic isolation of The Man of the Hill, or the even more impoverished self-interest of the bulk of the characters in the book.

Western's timely arrival on the scene of the intended rape of his daughter is an interesting example of the conflict between good and evil in the book. Western is roaring drunk and oblivious of his lack of propriety in invading the house of a Lady of Quality and insulting a Lord, but had he been less of a natural man unaware of social etiquette he would not have rescued Sophia from the unnatural designs of Lord Fellamar and Lady Bellaston. The rescue is a transparent contrivance by the author to protect his heroine but it is also credibly explained as the result of self-interested interference by Harriet Fitzpatrick, who betrays Sophia's whereabouts in the hope (vain as it proves) that this will reconcile her to Sophia's family. This is another example of the virtuous characters in *Tom Jones* profiting from the multiplicity of schemes against them. These either cancel one another out, as Lady Bellaston's and Harriet's do here, or so complicate one another as to become counter-productive, as the combined assaults on Tom by Fitzpatrick, Fellamar's press-gang, and Blifil's bribed witnesses do later. In *Jonathan Wild* Fielding portrayed evil self-interest as self-defeating even when it attained its ends, since those ends were so meanly conceived and so basely procured that they were not worth having and brought little or no satisfaction to their possessor.[4] Since the villains in *Tom Jones* are less successful, though only just, we do not see their victories turn to ashes in their mouths, but there is a similar suggestion that while the good may not always be happy, partly because their very goodness leads to involvement with the often unfortunate affairs of others, nonetheless only the good are capable of experiencing happiness worthy of the name. If the book does not offer that pseudo-religious enticement to virtue and dissuasion from vice that the author finds to be comfortable but untrue, it does urge strongly that only the virtuous *can* be happy, indeed only the virtuous can be fully human in the sense defined by the quotation from Terence of being able to experience the full range of human emotions. Even the most human of the bad characters are two-dimensional by comparison with the central trio. Not only are they unable to bring their schemes to fruition, but they are unable to convince the reader that they would much enjoy them if they could. Blifil might have gained Sophia and Allworthy's estates, but they would not have made him happy. Fielding has chosen a difficult task in portraying evil as at once threatening and self-defeating, omnipresent and impotent, but if he successfully demonstrates his thesis at the cost of somewhat limited characterization, I think he would be content with the bargain, though not all his readers perhaps would agree.

At the end of Book Fifteen, Tom begins to extricate himself from his entanglement with Lady Bellaston. Mistaken principles of gallantry led him into the affair, and it is not without poetic justice that his incompetence as a gallant precipitates his rejection of her. Lady Bellaston is announced by Partridge while Tom is hearing from Mrs Honour of Sophia's return to the custody of her father. Caught in a situation that Wycherley's Horner would not only have coped with but enjoyed, Tom is quite unequal to the challenge. In an earlier scene (XIV, ii) he had hurried Lady Bellaston behind the bed when Mrs Honour arrived, and she was obliged to hear from there the servants' gossip about her

[4] In his Preface to the *Miscellanies*, Fielding says of *Jonathan Wild*: 'it is, I believe, impossible to give Vice a true Relish of Honour and Glory, or tho' we give it Riches and Power, to give it the Enjoyment of them'; *Miscellanies*, p. 13. The argument is developed at length in *The Champion*, January 24, 1739–40; Henley, Vol. XV, pp. 165–9.

disreputable house of assignation. Tom has not, however, learned from this mistake, and when the ladies' roles are reversed he foolishly conceals Honour behind the bed, where she can hear his meeting with Lady Bellaston:

> *Honour* knew nothing of any Acquaintance that subsisted between him and Lady *Bellaston*, and she was almost the last Person in the World to whom he would have communicated it. In this Hurry and Distress, he took (as is common enough) the worst Course, and instead of exposing her to the Lady, which would have been of little Consequence, he chose to expose the Lady to her. (XV, vii; 809–10)

When Lady Bellaston has thoroughly compromised herself by her advances to Tom, Nightingale arrives dead drunk at Tom's door, driving Lady Bellaston in turn to seek refuge behind the curtains, where she discovers Honour. If Tom lacks presence of mind, she does not, and after her first fury she prudently buys Honour's silence by offering her a job. These comic and rather stagy discovery scenes lighten the oppressive atmosphere of the Bellaston connection. Tom's spirits are raised the next day when Nightingale repays some of his debt to Tom by acquainting him with Lady Bellaston's true character. This has a similar effect to that of the discovery that Will Barnes and not Tom had been Molly's first and favourite lover and the father of her child:

> Indeed he began to look on all the Favours he had received, rather as Wages than Benefits, which depreciated not only her, but himself too in his own Conceit, and put him quite out of Humour with both. (XV, ix; 819)

Nightingale also suggests to Tom the expedient of proposing marriage as a means of ending the relationship, a ploy which achieves its purpose but which Tom pays for later when the letter is shown to Sophia to discredit him further. Even at such a price, however, Tom is well out of so degrading a liaison.

His first chance to demonstrate that he has finally learned his lesson is the offer of marriage he receives from Mrs Hunt shortly after he has broken with Lady Bellaston. He is tempted by the lady herself, whom 'he liked ... as well as he did any Woman except *Sophia*', by her fortune, which 'would have been exceeding convenient to him', and by the notion of renouncing Sophia for her own good:

> Would it not be kinder to her, than to continue her longer engaged in a hopeless Passion for him? Ought he not to do so in Friendship to her? This Notion prevailed some Moments, and he had almost determined to be false to her from a high Point of Honour; but that Refinement was not able to stand very long against the Voice of Nature, which cried in his Heart, that such Friendship was Treason to Love. (XV, xi; 827)

Like Sophia when she was tempted by pride to make herself a martyr to duty and her father's wishes, Tom is here tempted by a theory about behaviour which bears little relationship to genuine human feelings, and which is consequently unable, in both cases, to stand very long against those feelings. The author does not comment further on Tom's action at the time, but later he makes his opinion clear:

> That refined Degree of *Platonic* Affection which is absolutely detached from the Flesh, and is indeed entirely and purely spiritual, is a Gift confined to the female Part of the Creation; many of whom I have heard declare, (and doubtless with great Truth) that they would, with the utmost Readiness, resign a Lover to a Rival, when such Resignation was proved to be necessary for the temporal Interest of such Lover. Hence, therefore, I conclude, that this Affection is in Nature, though I cannot pretend to say, I have ever seen an Instance of it. (XVI, v; 852)

Jane Austen's Emma is also briefly tempted to resign Knightley in favour of her 'infinitely... most worthy' friend Harriet, but a moment's consideration convinces her that: 'as to any of that heroism of sentiment... Emma had it not'.[5] Tom's love for Sophia similarly cuts through such attitudinizing and ensures that he will not look to his own and Sophia's 'temporal Interest' and marry Arabella Hunt. He has clearly changed since he unthinkingly accepted both Lady Bellaston's challenge to gallantry and her money. Like Lady Bellaston, Molly and Mrs Waters, Mrs Hunt is the initiator. Her offer, made in a letter to Tom, is altogether more attractive than Lady Bellaston's, though she does not appeal directly to his sexual enthusiasm by trying to seduce him as his other partners had done. Tom is thus more tempted by the idea but less by the prospect of immediate physical gratification. And marriage, if more respectable, represents a premeditated and permanent renunciation of Sophia, which casual liaisons do not. It might therefore be argued that

---

[5] R. W. Chapman (ed.), *The Novels of Jane Austen*, Vol. IV, London 1933, p. 431.

Tom's rejection of Mrs Hunt's offer is a less than entirely convincing demonstration that he would resist a purely sexual betrayal of Sophia. In the following books, however, he is given the chance to show that his change is a complete one. When Tom praises Sophia to her cousin Harriet the lady appropriates the sentiments to herself and tries to seduce him. But though she has the advantages of being young, available and accomplished, she fails to persuade Tom even to see her again:

> *Jones* then, after many Expressions of Thanks, very respectfully retired; nor could Mrs. *Fitzpatrick* forbear making him a Present of a Look at parting, by which if he had understood nothing, he must have had no Understanding in the Language of the Eyes. In Reality it confirmed his Resolution of returning to her no more; for faulty as he hath hitherto appeared in this History, his whole Thoughts were now so confined to his *Sophia*, that I believe no Woman upon Earth could have now drawn him into an Act of Inconstancy. (XVI, ix; 871)

As Tom is leaving this meeting with Harriet he is challenged by her husband. He ends up in prison for supposedly killing Fitzpatrick in the ensuing duel, and he is there visited by Mrs Waters who has been living with Fitzpatrick in the place of his wife. When she informs him that Fitzpatrick is out of danger Tom is greatly relieved. But when she ridicules his repentance with 'some Witticisms about *the Devil when he was sick*', and makes it apparent that she would welcome a resumption of their relations at Upton, Tom is not to be drawn, and their conversation:

> ended at last with perfect Innocence, and much more to the Satisfaction of *Jones* than of the Lady: For the former was greatly transported with the News she had brought him; but the latter was not altogether so pleased with the penitential Behaviour of a Man whom she had at her first Interview conceived a very different Opinion of from what she now entertained of him. (XVII, ix; 912)

Tom has been more celebrated for his three lapses than for his three subsequent rejections of overtures in the last part of the book. The number is not insignificant. In matching his yieldings to temptation with a similar number of resistances the author is confirming the change in his behaviour, as well as creating one of the many symmetries which structure *Tom Jones*, and one which has passed, I think, unnoticed. Penitence makes for duller reading than crime, as Defoe remarked in the Preface to *Moll Flanders*:

it is too true that the difference lies not in the real worth of the subject so much as in the gust and palate of the reader.[6]

Fielding might complain with more justice that his readers' enthusiasm for vice has led them to misread the true balance of vice and virtue in Tom's sexual behaviour.

It is not only Tom's affair with Lady Bellaston which brings him to the lowest ebb of his fortunes in London. His imprisonment in the Gatehouse for wounding Fitzpatrick, albeit in self-defence, is a punishment for his earlier, mistaken decision to defend his 'honour' as a soldier by duelling with Northerton. It is presumably the sword he bought on that occasion that he uses to fight Fitzpatrick. In addition to these two incidents the author has contrived a third, dramatic demonstration of his distaste for duelling. When Squire Western interrupts Lord Fellamar's attempt to rape Sophia a comedy of errors ensues in which Western urges Sophia to marry Blifil, while Lady Bellaston and Lord Fellamar assume that Fellamar is to be her husband. The misunderstanding is clarified in the following confrontation:

> 'Sir, I am Lord *Fellamar*,' answered he, 'and am the happy Man, whom I hope you have done the Honour of accepting for a Son-in-law.'
> 'You are a Son of a B——,' replied the Squire, 'for all your laced Coat. You my Son-in-Law, and be d——nd to you!'
> 'I shall take more from you, Sir, than from any Man,' answered the Lord; 'but I must inform you, that I am not used to hear such Language without Resentment.'
> 'Resent my A——,' quoth the Squire. 'Don't think I am afraid of such a Fellow as thee art? Because hast a got a Spit there dangling at thy Side. Lay by your Spit and I'll give thee enough of meddling with what doth not belong to thee.——I'll teach you to Father-in-law me. I'll lick thy Jacket.' (XV, v; 801)

Fellamar here behaves faultlessly according to the code of honour, but Western has the better of him. It is a situation not unknown in Restoration comedy in which the bumpkin squire, for all his uncouthness, sees the truth of the matter, while his town opponent is blinkered by his very sophistication.[7] Western is willing to fight, but not with lethal

---

[6] Juliet Mitchell (ed.), Harmondsworth 1978, p. 29.
[7] See, e.g., the encounter between Witwoud and his brother Sir Wilfull in Act Three of *The Way of the World*, Kathleen M. Lynch (ed.), London 1965, pp. 70–2.

weapons. When he is later waited upon by Fellamar's officious second there is another comic confrontation between the natural man and the artificial code of honour:

> 'Come down into Yard this Minute, and I'll take a Bout with thee at single Stick for a broken Head, that I will; or I will go into naked Room and box thee for a Belly full. At unt half a Man, at unt I'm sure.'
> The Captain, with some Indignation, replied, 'I see, Sir, you are below my Notice, and I shall inform his Lordship you are below his.' (XVI, ii; 837)

This splendid comedy of manners is not without its moral: Western though by no means simply admirable is right in this case and Fellamar and his lieutenant are wrong, and if Tom had adopted Western's approach with Fitzpatrick, he would not have ended in gaol with a man's blood on his conscience. If there is a degree of fear in Western's refusal to duel, it springs from an instinct for self-preservation which is a good deal saner and more humane than the stylized posturings of those who follow the code, and by the end of the book Tom has learned this along with his other, hard-won wisdom. The codes of honour and gallantry prescribe responses which are less than adequate to the situations in which Tom finds himself. Perhaps because they belong to the false sophistication of London, rather than the country where Tom has grown up, they distort his natural behaviour. And yet Western is more persuasive as a representative of this world because of his obvious limitations, just as Tom is better able to persuade Nightingale to marry Nancy because of his own misdemeanours. There are no 'Models of Perfection' (526) in *Tom Jones*, but those mixed characters who are portrayed are drafted into the service of virtue, and illustrate it better because of their faults.

Tom's ultimate reformation needs to be seen against this background. Since he had not the ability to judge intuitively, if he had not made mistakes of judgement, he could not have learned the salutary lessons to be derived from making mistakes and paying for them. The fact that he does pay for them and learn from them has not always been recognized. Ford Madox Ford, for example, suggests in the comment we have already looked at that Tom is rewarded *because* of his errors, and not because he has learned to overcome them:

> fellows like Fielding ... who pretend that if you are a gay drunkard, lecher, squanderer of your goods and fumbler in placket-holes you will eventually find a benevolent uncle, concealed father or benefactor who will shower on you bags of tens of thousands of guineas, estates and

the hands of adorable mistresses . . . are dangers to the body-politic and horribly bad constructors of plots.[8]

This may be an ironic use against Fielding of the *post hoc ergo propter hoc* argument he had used so amusingly against *Pamela* in *Shamela*, but it seriously distorts the very different morality of *Tom Jones*. The criticism of the plot is particularly misleading, since a good deal of the intricate plotting of the last six books is concerned with bringing down upon Tom the unfortunate consequences of his misdeeds. While the counterplots eventually extricate him from his misfortunes, they do so only after the experience of those misfortunes has convinced him that the follies of youth are not to be as casually shrugged off as Ford suggests. Tom spends almost all of the last six books wrestling unsuccessfully with what seems to be his fate, and he has need of his sanguine temper to keep him from despair. If he takes pleasure from again being close to Sophia, it is at the expense of being constantly reminded that he cannot possess her without ruining her. If he takes pleasure in uniting Nightingale and Nancy, the pleasure is tempered by reflecting that his own love match cannot end thus happily. If he enjoys the favours of Lady Bellaston, they are not such as to excite much appetite:

> Such was the unhappy case of *Jones*; for tho' the virtuous Love which he bore to *Sophia*, and which left very little Affection for any other Woman, had been entirely out of the Question, he could never have been able to have made an adequate Return to the generous Passion of this Lady, who had indeed been once an Object of Desire; but was now entered at least into the Autumn of Life; though she wore all the Gayety of Youth both in her Dress and Manner; nay, she contrived still to maintain the Roses in her Cheeks; but these, like Flowers forced out of Season by Art, had none of that lively blooming Freshness with which Nature, at the proper Time, bedecks her own Productions. She had, besides, a certain Imperfection, which renders some Flowers, tho' very beautiful to the Eye, very improper to be placed in a Wilderness of Sweets, and what above all others is most disagreeable to the Breath of Love. (XIII, ix; 724)

This description makes it clear that Tom's service to the lady is no gay fumbling in placket-holes, and very little lechery, but rather a duty enforced by the debt he feels he owes her. There is in fact no suggestion in the book that Tom finds making love to Lady Bellaston anything other

---

[8] *The English Novel*, pp. 99–100.

than irksome and unpleasant. The flower and seasonal imagery used to describe their relations expresses physical distaste discreetly but unmistakeably. Tom is nonetheless plagued by the consequences of his mistaken gallantry for most of his time in London, and this despite the fact that he releases himself from Lady Bellaston as soon as he decently can and refuses any further sexual involvement for the remainder of the book.

At the beginning of Book Eighteen, immediately after Tom has rejected the renewed advances of Mrs Waters, Partridge, who has seen the lady for the first time, tells Tom that he had slept with his mother at Upton. Tom's belief that he has been guilty of incest is a delayed nemesis, but one which comes upon him at a low point in his fortunes and plunges him into despair. The author introduces the incest scare somewhat abruptly, like the proposal from Mrs Hunt, and they are both whisked off-stage as quickly as they had been brought on. Tom's response to Partridge's information marks the final stage of his reformation:

> 'Sure,' cries *Jones*, 'Fortune will never have done with me, till she hath driven me to Distraction. But why do I blame Fortune? I am myself the Cause of all my Misery. All the dreadful Mischiefs which have befallen me, are the Consequences only of my own Folly and Vice.' (XVIII, ii; 915–16)

This accepting of responsibility for his actions and their consequences marks the beginning of true prudence in Tom. Whether it is a sudden insight or the first articulation of a growing awareness it represents a mature and morally responsible attitude. While Tom has always been capable of this he has demonstrated it only intermittently before, and then usually in others' affairs not his own. When he is rewarded with Sophia's hand and Allworthy's estate at the end of the book it is not because of or even in spite of the errors he here acknowledges, but because his experience of their consequences has taught him not to repeat them.

The change in Tom is both sudden and prepared for. In Fielding's *Pasquin* the author Trapwit claims that his comic denouement:

> is done, slap all at once; and that too by an Incident arising from the main Business of the Play, and to which every thing conduces.[9]

The same might be said not only of the change in Tom's fortunes at the end of the book but also of the change in Tom himself. What a casual

---

[9] Henry Fielding, *Pasquin*, O. M. Brack, Jr, William Kupersmith and Curt A. Zimansky (eds), Iowa City 1973, p. 11.

reader may mistake for a fifth-act conversion will be seen to be inevitable by the reader who reflects on the stages of Tom's progress towards wisdom.

The last six books of *Tom Jones* are crammed with action, the pace accelerating from the comparatively leisurely to the decidedly hectic, but the author continues his practice of writing reflective introductory chapters to each book. Book Fourteen opens with a discussion of the need for writers to have some knowledge of what they write about, the specific example being 'the Manners of upper Life' which 'many *English* Writers have totally failed in describing' because 'in Reality they know nothing of it' (XIV, i; 741). In the author's view:

> the highest Life is much the dullest, and affords very little Humour or Entertainment . . . except among the few who are engaged in the Pursuit of Ambition, and the fewer still who have a Relish for Pleasure, all is Vanity and servile Imitation. Dressing and Cards, eating and drinking, bowing and curtesying, make up the Business of their Lives. (743)

Lady Bellaston, we are told, is far from typical in her intrepid pursuit of pleasure:

> I am convinced there never was less of Love Intrigue carried on among Persons of Condition, than now. Our present Women have been taught by their Mothers to fix their Thoughts only on Ambition and Vanity, and to despise the Pleasures of Love as unworthy their Regard; and being afterwards, by the Care of such Mothers, married without having Husbands, they seem pretty well confirmed in the Justness of those Sentiments. (743)

This effects an important refocusing of the reader's view of London society. Lady Bellaston, its principal representative, is atypical in her determined and unscrupulous pursuit of sexual gratification. Tom is seduced and almost press-ganged at her instigation, and Sophia put in danger of rape, but the main threat that the rest of London society represents for the protagonists is the false ideology of love which Mrs Western and the family try to force upon Sophia, and which would result in disappointment and boredom rather than violence. The author's vision of evil comprises a Scylla of active malevolence and a Charybdis of passive vacuity, and it is the task of Tom and Sophia to avoid both. Tom is more consistently subjected to the former, in the plottings of Blifil and

Lady Bellaston, and Sophia to the latter, in the marriage schemes of her father and her aunt, but Sophia must face the physical threat of Fellamar, and Tom must resist the temptation of pragmatic self-interest posed by Mrs Hunt.

In the last third of *Tom Jones* there is more potentially 'tragical' material than before. The author describes both the attempted rape of Sophia and the apparent incest committed by Tom as tragical (XV, iv; 796 & XVIII, ii; 915), and in the introductory chapter to Book Seventeen he plays with the alternate possibilities of ending his work comically and tragically. He suggests that the affairs of Tom and Sophia are in so parlous a condition that he may not be able to extricate them without violating the rules of probability. This latter is an excellent example of the use of the introductory chapters, and other authorial passages, to maintain the tone and detachment of comedy when the narrative threatens to become tragic. The description of the dullness of high life in London in the earlier introductory chapter has the same effect. Comedy requires that the plots against the lovers by the forces of evil should threaten serious harm without ever really being likely to accomplish it, and that the evil characters themselves should ultimately prove to be less convincing, less entirely human, than the good. Fielding achieves this balance by involving the reader in the narrative and then detaching him from it with authorial comments, so that while he is involved in the fate of Tom and Sophia and concerned that they win through he also knows that they will. The detachment of the author signals that this is a comedy which, like all proper comedies, will end with the marriage of the lovers. But if the final triumph of the good over the evil is inevitable, it is certainly neither easy nor automatic, and it is stressed throughout *Tom Jones* that what must happen in art is by no means certain in life. Much of the complexity of the book comes from the interaction between the author's comic view of the world, and the intractable evil of much of human nature as he sees it. In the microcosm of the book he can ensure that the best of human nature is properly celebrated and rewarded, but he takes the trouble to point out that in the macrocosm it is often otherwise, in this life at least.

The final introductory chapter of *Tom Jones* deserves special mention. The denouement in the last two books is particularly involved and fast-moving, so much so that the author keeps his chapter-headings minimal and unobtrusive, those in Book Eighteen being confined to stating that the story is continuing or is approaching its end. Between the last two books, however, the author makes his last and one of his most characteristic personal appearances:

> We are now, Reader, arrived at the last Stage of our long Journey. As we have therefore travelled together through so many Pages, let us behave to one another like Fellow-Travellers in a Stage-Coach, who have passed several Days in the Company of each other; and who, notwithstanding any Bickerings or little Animosities which may have occurred on the Road, generally make all up at last, and mount, for the last Time, into their Vehicle with Chearfulness and Good-Humour; since, after this one Stage, it may possibly happen to us, as it commonly happens to them, never to meet more. (XVIII, i; 913)

This is a fine example of how the author's familiar style is used to dramatize the act of reading into a personal relationship between author and reader. The stage-coach analogy, which is particularly appropriate to a book full of journeys and dinners, depicts the proximity of author and reader during their shared experience of *Tom Jones*. It suggests the interchange of ideas, the two-way dialogue, which can occur in oral narration but only by imaginative extension in a written work. The author resists the impersonal nature of written fiction and persistently tries to project the feeling of being face to face with his audience, like an actor in the theatre, not shut off alone in his study, writing. The tone, adapted to the imagined situation, is courteous, cheerful, and good-humoured. The author, as befits a fellow traveller, is neither too distant nor too insinuating. He does not understate differences of interest in his effort to reconcile them and lest any misunderstandings remain he puts aside the various rhetorical stances he has adopted:

> Now it is well known, that all Jokes and Raillery are at this Time laid aside; whatever Characters any of the Passengers have for the Jest-sake personated on the Road, are now thrown off, and the Conversation is usually plain and serious. (913)

The last third of *Tom Jones* began with the author writing personally about the depiction of the real worth of Charlotte Fielding under the fictional name of Sophia, and about 'the little Parlour' in which he wrote, inspired by the hope of fame and the need for money (XIII, i; 683). The last introductory chapter is also personal, but the jesting has been replaced by a plain and serious defence of his character:

> I question not but thou hast been told, among other Stories of me, that thou wast to travel with a very scurrilous Fellow: But whoever told thee so, did me an Injury. No Man detests and despises Scurrility more than myself; nor hath any Man more Reason; for none hath ever been treated with more. (914)

The personal abuse Fielding suffered in his lifetime has long since faded, but the critical reception of his work is still sometimes hostile and dismissive. William Empson suggests that: 'the chief reason why recent critics have belittled Fielding is that they find him intimidating'.[10] Fielding's author certainly evolves into a complex, fascinating, and in some ways formidable presence by the end of the book. (I hesitate to call him a character, because he is both more and less than an ordinary fictional character.) He speaks truth with a smiling countenance, often enclosing his sentiments in single, double, or multiple irony, and he expects the most capable of his readers to follow this rhetoric, and to seek out the book's doctrine. Readers who choose to engage fully with the book will find its author demanding, but too companionable to be intimidating. Indeed his geniality, lightness of touch, and self-deprecating humour may have contributed to his being misinterpreted as morally shallow and flippant. It would be difficult, however, to mistake the straightforward warmth of the 'Farewel to the Reader', with its concern to dismiss false reports and to set matters straight with the reader.

One of the characters most often misunderstood is Allworthy, who reappears in Book Sixteen. His arrival in London with Blifil is preceded by an account of his generosity to Mrs Miller, who is put in the difficult position of having to turn out her benefactor Tom, and her new son-in-law Nightingale, or refuse accommodation to her benefactor Allworthy, with whom she has a standing arrangement:

> When he settled the Annuity of 50 *l.* a Year, therefore, on Mrs. *Miller*, he told her, 'It was in Consideration of always having her First-Floor when he was in Town,' (which he scarce ever intended to be) 'but that she might let it at any other Time, for that he would always send her a Month's Warning.' He was now, however, hurried to Town so suddenly, that he had no Opportunity of giving such Notice. (XV, x; 822–3)

Tom comes to her rescue by suggesting that he and the Nightingales move to Nightingale's new lodging, and allow Allworthy to have his usual rooms. The scene is a small one, but a touchstone of generous and punctilious behaviour by Tom, Allworthy, and Mrs Miller, of whom it is said: 'Nothing short of the Fair and Honourable will satisfy the Delicacy of their Minds' (823). The author often places such scenes, which remind the reader of the admirable qualities of Allworthy and Tom, immediately

---

[10] 'Tom Jones' in Paulson (ed.), *Fielding: A Collection of Critical Essays*, p. 145.

before he shows them doing something mistaken. In the present instance, the account of Allworthy's unobtrusive generosity to Mrs Miller precedes a long explanation of how he is deceived by Blifil, who persuades him to support the furthering of his suit to Sophia, when her running away has indicated pretty clearly her dislike for the match. The explanation begins with this account of Blifil's motives:

> As the Love which *Blifil* had for *Sophia* was of that violent Kind, which nothing but the Loss of her Fortune, or some such Accident, could lessen, his Inclination to the Match was not at all altered by her having run away, though he was obliged to lay this to his own Account . . . he now proposed the Gratification of a very strong Passion besides Avarice, by marrying this young Lady, and this was Hatred. (XVI, vi; 858)

As Allworthy cannot be expected to second so base a design, he has to be deceived, both about Blifil's supposed affection for Sophia, and about the likelihood of her coming to return that affection which, given her extreme avoiding action, hardly seems likely. He is eventually persuaded to allow Blifil to renew his suit, though he insists that Sophia must be 'brought freely to Compliance' (860) before he will consent to a marriage, and the author comments on the success of Blifil's deception:

> Thus did the Affection of *Allworthy* for his Nephew, betray the superior Understanding to be triumphed over by the inferiour; and thus is the Prudence of the best of Heads often defeated by the Tenderness of the best of Hearts. (860)

The entire passage is typical of the method of *Tom Jones*. The incident by itself would make Allworthy look at least a dupe and at worst a fool. The author's detailed explanation and careful rhetoric, however, eventually so modify the reader's assessment that he can endorse the final summary that the best of hearts may overcome the best of heads. But a reader anxious to get on with the story, to find out what happens and to draw his own conclusions, is inclined to skip or to slur over the painstaking authorial interpretation, to deduce that Allworthy is a fool, and that the author foolishly tries to palliate his folly instead of making him more perceptive. This common misreading of Fielding overlooks one of his central perceptions of the nature of goodness: that of its very nature it is innocent and open to deception by practised hypocrisy.

Mrs Miller, who joins the select band of the good in the last third of the book, is typically innocent in this way:

> This poor Creature might indeed be called Simplicity itself. She was one of that Order of Mortals, who are apt to believe every thing which is said to them; to whom Nature hath neither indulged the offensive nor defensive Weapons of Deceit, and who are consequently liable to be imposed upon by any one, who will only be at the Expence of a little Falshood for that Purpose. (XVII, viii; 905)

While the other admirable characters are less simple than Mrs Miller, they share, to a greater or less degree, her openness and lack of defence. Sophia, who is naturally wise, is the least open to deception; Tom has to learn by experience how often appearances deceive; and Allworthy, though he has had a good deal of experience, is still, like Tom, often deceived at first, though, also like Tom, he comes eventually to know the truth, and when he does his judgement is more just and less forgiving. Thwackum, for example, writes to Allworthy in London, abusing Tom and asking for a second Living. The author had earlier pointed out that Allworthy knew less of Thwackum than the author and the reader but his final assessment is just:

> This was the first Time *Thwackum* ever wrote in this authoritative Stile to *Allworthy*, and of this he had afterwards sufficient Reason to repent, as in the Case of those who mistake the highest Degree of Goodness for the lowest Degree of Weakness. *Allworthy* had indeed never liked this Man. (XVIII, iv; 929)

A good many readers as well as Thwackum have mistaken Allworthy's goodness for weakness. *Tom Jones* endeavours, as we have seen, to make good men wise to the deceptions to which their nature lays them open. If Tom and Allworthy were always as perceptive as Sophia, no dramatic illustration of this doctrine would be possible. Believing the doctrine, Fielding had to show his good men deceived while insisting that they were neither weak nor imperceptive. He gives the forces of evil plenty of rope, which not only enables the plot to function, but also allows a graphic demonstration of the dangers they pose before they succeed in hanging themselves. Tom almost comes to Tyburn, Sophia to a loveless marriage, and Allworthy to the avuncular patronage of a race of little Blifils. The author, as usual, is only half joking at the beginning of Book Seventeen when he suggests that he may have to end his book tragically. The tone of the preceding Books would have been quite different if that had been going to happen, but the plot, at least in its potentialities, could quite as easily have failed to rescue Tom and to enlighten Allworthy in time.

The greatest ally that Tom and Allworthy have is the inevitability in Fielding's comic world that with time the truth will emerge, often because those who conspire to distort it are betrayed by one another. Immediately before he receives the final letter from Thwackum Allworthy receives a death-bed letter from Square. The two tutors are locked together in opposition even at this late stage, but the nature of their opposition has changed. While Thwackum continues to berate Tom and to pursue his self-interest, Square knows that he is dying and to ease his conscience he tells Allworthy the truth about Tom. He also relates his conversion from 'philosophy' to Christianity, and this, together with his thorough vindication of Tom's character, moves him at last to the side of the angels. It is interesting that it is Square and not Thwackum who is saved. In Fielding's world a tutor of uncertain belief and one prone to sexual indulgence is more to be trusted, finally, than one whose 'Life and Manners' exhibit 'strict Severity', and who has 'a most devout Attachment to Religion' (XVIII, iv; 929). Appearances, as ever, are deceptive, and the more upright a man appears, the more likely he is to be of the devil's party.

The conversion of Square, like the reformation of Tom, is open to the objection that characters do not change like this in life as opposed to art. In the twentieth century we have accepted a psychology which asserts that character is shaped in childhood and does not greatly change thereafter, and we therefore view with suspicion adult changes of mind and heart. Fielding, who did not share this assumption, would not have written a passionately moral book if he did not believe that those who read it might be changed by it. Modern literary conventions, which are based on our psychological beliefs, lead us to accept development or evolution in character, as Henry Knight Miller points out, but to reject the 'conversion' traditional in the romance in which a young man who had been indiscriminate in his pleasures might be abruptly matured by a realization of his true nature and purpose in life.[11] It should be emphasized that there is no easy sentimentality in Fielding's depiction of such changes. He sees, as he usually does, all round the issue and is himself caustic about unnatural, fifth-act conversions:

> Our modern Authors of Comedy have fallen almost universally into the Error here hinted at: Their Heroes generally are notorious Rogues, and their Heroines abandoned Jades, during the first four Acts; but in the fifth, the former become very worthy Gentlemen, and the latter,

---

[11] *Henry Fielding's 'Tom Jones' and the Romance Tradition*, p. 61.

Women of Virtue and Discretion: Nor is the Writer often so kind as to give himself the least Trouble, to reconcile or account for this monstrous Change and Incongruity. There is, indeed, no other Reason to be assigned for it, than because the Play is drawing to a Conclusion; as if it was no less natural in a Rogue to repent in the last Act of a Play, than in the last of his Life; which we perceive to be generally the case at *Tyburn*, a Place which might, indeed, close the Scene of some Comedies with much Propriety, as the Heroes in these are most commonly eminent for those very Talents which not only bring Men to the Gallows, but enable them to make an heroic Figure when they are there. (VIII, i; 406)

The sentimentality which saved Macheath at the end of *The Beggar's Opera*, which transformed Jonathan Wild from a spiv into a folk hero, and which lionized criminals who went to the gallows defiantly, is here specifically excluded from *Tom Jones*. Though he is threatened with Tyburn, Tom is no rogue. His thoughts are not on how he might appear bravely at the place of execution but rather on the folly and vice which have led to his imprisonment and for which he accepts responsibility. He sees that the principles of 'honour' and 'gallantry' he accepted from his society have led him into immoral behaviour and he rejects them. The change in Tom is one of perception, not of moral character. It is Tom's very virtue which troubles Square's conscience. In his hour of crisis Tom's good deeds rise up to support him, and he is saved, ultimately, as he is changed, by his essential goodness. The morality of his author and the entire doctrine of *Tom Jones* rest upon the reader's being convinced of this.

What develops in *Tom Jones* is not character but plot. The highly complex and elaborate denouement of the last two books serves to demonstrate that Tom is rescued by his own virtue and not simply by authorial fiat. The author prefaces the denouement with a statement of this principle:

> I faithfully promise, that notwithstanding any Affection which we may be supposed to have for this Rogue, whom we have unfortunately made our Heroe, we will lend him none of that supernatural Assistance with which we are entrusted, upon Condition that we use it only on very important Occasions. If he doth not therefore find some natural Means of fairly extricating himself from all his Distresses, we will do no Violence to the Truth and Dignity of History for his Sake; for we had rather relate that he was hanged at *Tyburn* (which may very probably be the Case) than forfeit our Integrity, or shock the Faith of our Reader. (XVII, i; 875–6)

The mock-solemn tone of this passage lightens its impact, but the author is nonetheless in earnest. The very next chapter is headed: 'The generous and grateful Behaviour of Mrs. *Miller*' (877), and it relates her staunch defence of Tom to Allworthy when Blifil gleefully informs him that Tom has killed Fitzpatrick and is consequently 'one of the greatest Villains upon Earth' (877). Mrs Miller is Tom's chief advocate with Allworthy and Sophia in the last books, and what she lacks in sophistication she more than makes up for in single-minded enthusiasm for his cause. Having witnessed a signal instance of Tom's disinterested goodness in furthering the marriage of Nancy and Nightingale, she refuses to let anything get in the way of her sure judgement of that action and her determination to repay it. And as so often with other characters in the book, she is persuasive because of her limitations, not despite them.

She is aided by Fitzpatrick, who tells the truth about his fight with Tom, and by the successive disclosures of Partridge, Mrs Waters and Lawyer Dowling, who between them finally unravel the truth of Tom's parentage, and the extent of Blifil's plotting against him. While these are all elegantly interlocked, nothing that happens to extricate Tom from his distresses is unnatural; indeed, there is a fine inevitability about the process of his restoration to the favour of Allworthy and Sophia. At the beginning of Book Seventeen, however, the action is so finely poised that the same chain of events which eventually rescues Tom seems more than likely to lead him to Tyburn, and the plot of the book thus emphasizes its ambiguity and its juxtaposition of nature and artifice. The author who draws the reader's attention to his skilful plotting can in his next breath assert that what happens is natural:

> If the Reader will please to refresh his Memory, by turning to the Scene at *Upton* in the Ninth Book, he will be apt to admire the many strange Accidents which unfortunately prevented any Interview between *Partridge* and Mrs. *Waters*, when she spent a whole Day there with Mr. *Jones*. Instances of this Kind we may frequently observe in Life, where the greatest Events are produced by a nice Train of little Circumstances; and more than one Example of this may be discovered by the accurate Eye, in this our History. (XVIII, ii; 916)

Bergson defined the comic as: 'any arrangement of acts and events... which gives us, in a single combination, the illusion of life and the distinct impression of a mechanical arrangement',[12] and this is precisely what

---

[12] *Laughter: An Essay on the Meaning of the Comic*, trans. C. Brereton and F. Rothwell, London 1911, p. 69.

happens in *Tom Jones*. The ending of the plot is simultaneously a triumph of nature and a triumph of art, with the author careful as always to distinguish between them, so that they may truly complement one another. In life Tom may well have been hanged, but in art he is rescued, naturally, because he deserves to be, and the reader is left to ponder the implications of this disparity. It is appropriate in a comic work that the structural mechanism should be only partly concealed by the illusion it supports and that a real tension should be maintained between them, so that the reader is never able either to submit completely to the illusion or to withdraw completely from it. The action must both unfold in a lifelike manner and appear a picture of life composed and framed by the author. And the author must stay in his heaven because the comic vision demands that his providential care for his created world be apparent.

As the book draws towards its close and the many components of the narrative fall into place with precision, the pleasures of closure, which the plot supplies abundantly, are mixed with the sense of loss that accompanies the ending of all great literary works whether comic or tragic. Both emotions colour the final reconciliation scene between Tom and Sophia. It is a crucial scene: as well as reuniting the lovers prior to their marriage, it gives Sophia and the reader a chance to judge the reformed Tom. The plot of the book has by now answered the question 'who is Tom?', but the thematic question 'what is Tom?' is not concluded until Sophia and the reader are entirely convinced that he is a worthy husband for her. While in some senses Tom has always been so, in others he has to make his reformation credible. Sophia, who has not seen the process of that reformation, as the reader has, is cautious. A young woman of unusual judgement, she both wants to be reconciled to her lover and refuses to be so until she is genuinely convinced that his character is amended.

After some brief but important introductory comments by the author the scene is presented dramatically. Tom, who has had his share of criticism, now receives some direct compliments:

> He was indeed one of the finest Figures ever beheld, and his Person alone would have charmed the greater Part of Womankind; but we hope it hath already appeared in this History, that Nature, when she formed him, did not totally rely, as she sometimes doth, on this Merit only, to recommend her Work. (XVIII, xii; 970)

Sophia, who has been so patently Tom's superior in prudence and virtue, is teased a little:

> *Sophia*, who, angry as she was, was likewise set forth to the best Advantage, for which I leave my female Readers to account, appeared so extremely beautiful . . . (970)

Before they bustle out to leave the lovers alone Allworthy calls Sophia 'the finest Creature in the World' and Western responds: 'So much the better for *Tom*;—for d--n me if he shan't ha the tousling her'. The emphasis on Sophia's worth, on the physical attractiveness of both the lovers, and on the sexual pleasures which will follow a reconciliation, sets the stage for what follows in which these factors are the controlling ones. It is not inappropriate that the introduction to the scene should serve to put the lovers more on a level than they have been, by reminding the reader of Tom's attractiveness, and of Sophia's feminine failings. An authorial tone of benign amusement, which continues throughout the ensuing scene, is established in these comments and in the ironic observation which follows:

> The Lovers were now alone, and it will, I question not, appear strange to many Readers, that those who had so much to say to one another when Danger and Difficulty attended their Conversation, and who seemed so eager to rush into each others Arms when so many Bars lay in their Way, now that with Safety they were at Liberty to say or do whatever they pleased, should both remain for some Time silent and motionless; insomuch, that a Stranger of moderate Sagacity might have well concluded they were mutually indifferent. (971)

Though unexpected, their shyness is natural and forms an amusing contrast to the lively dialogue which follows when the ice is broken. As the lovers thaw, the commentary turns to drama: shyness must be told, while dialogue may be shown.

When he can speak, Tom begins by asking for mercy not justice for his past transgressions and by asserting that: 'No Repentance was ever more sincere' (972). Sophia answers in a manner which illustrates the epitome of prudence as defined throughout *Tom Jones*:

> 'Sincere Repentance, Mr. *Jones*,' answered she, 'will obtain the Pardon of a Sinner, but it is from one who is a perfect Judge of that Sincerity. A human Mind may be imposed on; nor is there any infallible Method to prevent it. You must expect however, that if I can be prevailed on by your Repentance to pardon you, I will at least insist on the strongest Proof of its Sincerity.' (972)

This is justice tempered with mercy. Justice as well as prudence demands that Tom's repentance not only be sincere, but be seen by fallible human judges to give satisfactory evidence of sincerity. Mercy requires that some hope be held out to Tom to sustain him through the period in which he is to demonstrate this sincerity in actions as well as words: 'After what is past, Sir, can you expect I should take you upon your Word?' Tom's reply is a splendid piece of courtroom rhetoric. He takes the initiative from Sophia by offering 'a better Security, a Pledge for my Constancy, which it is impossible to see and to doubt' (973), and then leads her to a mirror:

> There, behold it there, in that lovely Figure, in that Face, that Shape, those Eyes, that Mind which shines through those Eyes: Can the Man who shall be in Possession of these be inconstant? Impossible! my *Sophia*. They would fix a *Dorimant*, a Lord *Rochester*. You could not doubt it, if you could see yourself with any Eyes but your own.

All is fair in love, and in court, and Tom's argument is persuasive, though it is a good deal more *ad feminam* than *ad rem*. Sophia, unfairly appealed to, remains cool enough to rebuke Tom for a sexist distinction:

> 'The Delicacy of your Sex cannot conceive the Grossness of ours, nor how little one Sort of Amour has to do with the Heart.' 'I will never marry a Man,' replied *Sophia*, very gravely, 'who shall not learn Refinement enough to be as incapable as I am myself of making such a Distinction.' (973)

Tom is thus corrected, for the last time, for his separation of love and sex. It is apparent that he still has much to learn, and that while his repentance is sincere, he is not thereby rendered perfect, nor as wise and discriminating as Sophia. He is, however, willing to improve: '"I will learn it," said *Jones*, "I have learnt it already."' In remaining humanly fallible to the end, Tom illustrates precisely how he has changed. Accepting personal responsibility for his actions, and rejecting socially-accepted codes of behaviour in favour of unfashionable but genuinely moral choices, does make Tom mature, but it does not change his sanguine temper, his more than generous warmth, his lack of even a healthy suspicion, and his inability to use either the offensive or defensive weapons of deceit. He will always need the prudence of Sophia to guide him as it does in this scene. Even with it he will be open to mistakes of judgement of the kind that Allworthy makes in the book, since any human mind may be imposed upon. But the thoughtless follies of youth are behind him, and his reunion with Sophia and Allworthy ensures that he will have the best of human models and advice, which is the best that can be hoped for in a fallen world. Even in the midst of the happy ending, however, Fielding's vision of that world retains its essential duality: while Tom retires to domestic happiness in the country Blifil saves his money to purchase a seat in Parliament (XVIII, xiii; 979).

When Tom and Sophia have reached an essential understanding, Western rushes in, and the scene dissolves into good-humoured, and at times boisterous, comedy. Western uses his 'fatherly Authority' (975) to persuade Sophia to waive the trial period for Tom and to marry him the next day. The lovers behave with quiet joy, Allworthy with decorous affability, and Western, as always, with crude enthusiasm. Tom's final happiness comes hard upon his earlier misfortunes, but this is not merely a conventional happy ending. In Smollett's *Roderick Random*, published twelve months before *Tom Jones*, (and wrongly attributed by some contemporaries to Fielding) the hero also recovers his family and fortune, marries his one true love, and settles down to quiet and respectable family life in the country, but the similarities end there. Roderick is a true picaro, surviving by whatever means he can in a violent and hostile world. Though his adventures expose the evils of contemporary society, he is not himself much concerned with morality, and he experiences no change of heart, but only a change of fortune, at the end of the book. Tom's experiences are less extensive and less severe though still in many ways picaresque, but he is not a picaro. His recovery of family, fortune, and Sophia is not a chance turn of events but an earned reward for surviving, bloody but unbowed, his period of moral testing. Lest the reader mistake the sudden reversal of his fortunes for an unearned and arbitrary indulgence, the author adds a note on his subsequent behaviour:

> Whatever in the Nature of *Jones* had a Tendency to Vice, hath been corrected by continual Conversation with this good Man [Allworthy], and by his Union with the lovely and virtuous *Sophia*. He hath also, by Reflexion on his past Follies, acquired a Discretion and Prudence very uncommon in one of his lively Parts. (XVIII, xiii; 981)

If Tom is not obliged to demonstrate his reformation by a twelve-month trial before marriage, he is shown here to have amply demonstrated it in the years immediately following. The author is merciful to Tom, as Tom was merciful to Blifil and Black George, but justice is also served by this final description of his behaviour. Throughout *Tom Jones* the author has insisted, as Sophia says, that actions alone are a sure indication of a man's character, and it is therefore entirely appropriate that Tom should demonstrate the truth of his professions to Sophia by living up to them.

SELECT BIBLIOGRAPHY

A. Editions

The Complete Works of Henry Fielding, Esq. Ed. William E. Henley, 16 vols, Heinemann, London 1903; reissued Cass, London, and Barnes & Noble, New York 1967.
   This remains the best collected edition though it is inaccurate and incomplete. It is progressively being replaced by the altogether more authoritative Wesleyan Edition.

The following volumes of *The Wesleyan Edition of the Works of Henry Fielding* have appeared:

The History of Tom Jones: A Foundling. Ed. Martin C. Battestin and Fredson Bowers, 2 vols, Wesleyan University Press 1975, and Clarendon, Oxford 1974.
The History of Tom Jones: A Foundling. Ed. Martin C. Battestin and Fredson Bowers, Wesleyan University Press [1977].
   This one-volume edition, incorporating revisions and corrections, is the authoritative text.
Joseph Andrews. Ed. Martin C. Battestin, Clarendon, Oxford 1967.
Miscellanies by Henry Fielding, Esq; Volume One. Ed. Henry Knight Miller, Clarendon, Oxford 1972.
The Jacobite's Journal and Related Writings. Ed. W. B. Coley, Clarendon, Oxford 1974.

Other useful modern editions include:

The History of Tom Jones. Ed. R. P. C. Mutter, Penguin, Harmondsworth 1966.
Tom Jones. Ed. Sheridan Baker, Norton, New York 1973. This Norton Critical Edition includes selections of criticism from 1749 to 1968.
The Author's Farce. Ed. Charles B. Woods, Arnold, London 1967.
The Covent-Garden Journal. Ed. Gerald E. Jensen, 2 vols, Yale University Press, New Haven 1915; reissued Russell & Russell, New York 1964.
The Grub-Street Opera. Ed. Edgar V. Roberts, Arnold, London 1969.
The Historical Register For the Year 1736 and Eurydice Hissed. Ed. William W. Appleton, Arnold, London 1968.
Joseph Andrews and Shamela. Ed. Martin C. Battestin, Houghton Mifflin, Boston 1961.

Pasquin. Ed. O. M. Brack, Jr, William Kupersmith and Curt A. Zimansky, University of Iowa, Iowa City 1973.
Tom Thumb and The Tragedy of Tragedies. Ed. L. J. Morrissey, Oliver and Boyd, Edinburgh 1970.

B. BIBLIOGRAPHIES

New Cambridge Bibliography of English Literature, Vol. 2. Ed. George Watson, Cambridge University Press 1971.
    Includes the Fielding canon and a list of critical studies from 1744 to 1968.
See also Cross (*in* C *below*)

C. BIOGRAPHIES

Cross, Wilbur L., *The History of Henry Fielding*, 3 vols, Yale University Press, New Haven 1918; reissued Russell & Russell, New York 1963.
    Despite its errors this remains the standard biography.
Dudden, F. Homes, *Henry Fielding: His Life, Works, and Times*, 2 vols, Clarendon, Oxford 1952.
    Adds some useful background to Cross.

D. CRITICISM

The following is a selective list of some of the more useful studies.

Alter, Robert, *Fielding and the Nature of the Novel*. Harvard University Press, Cambridge, Mass. 1968.
    A very readable introduction to Fielding's art.
Baker, Sheridan, 'Bridget Allworthy: The Creative Pressures of Fielding's Plot'. *Papers of the Michigan Academy of Science, Arts, and Letters*, Vol. LII, 1967, pp. 345–56.
—, 'Henry Fielding and the Cliché'. *Criticism*, Vol. 1, 1959, pp. 354–61.
—, 'Henry Fielding's Comic Romances'. *Papers of the Michigan Academy of Science, Arts, and Letters*, Vol. XLV, 1960, pp. 411–19.
Battestin, Martin C., *The Moral Basis of Fielding's Art: A Study of Joseph Andrews*. Wesleyan University Press, Middletown, Conn. 1959.
    Documents Fielding's debt to the latitudinarian divines.
—, *The Providence of Wit: Aspects of Form in Augustan Literature and the Arts*. Clarendon, Oxford 1974.
    Includes two perceptive chapters on providence and wisdom in *Tom Jones*.
—, 'Osborne's *Tom Jones*: Adapting a Classic'. *Virginia Quarterly Review*, Vol. XLII, 1966, pp. 378–93.
    Compares the novel and Tony Richardson's 1964 film version.
—, 'Tom Jones and "His *Egyptian* Majesty": Fielding's Parable of Government'. *PMLA*, Vol. LXXXII, 1967, pp. 68–77.
—(ed.), *Twentieth Century Interpretations of Tom Jones*. Prentice-Hall, Englewood Cliffs, N.J. 1968.
    An excellent collection of modern essays.
Blanchard, Frederic T., *Fielding the Novelist: A Study in Historical Criticism*. Yale University Press, New Haven 1926; reissued Russell & Russell, New York 1966.
    A scholarly account of Fielding's reputation from 1742 to *c.* 1920.

Bronson, Bertrand H., 'Strange Relations: The Author and His Audience' in *Facets of the Enlightenment*. University of California Press, Berkeley and Los Angeles 1968, pp. 298-325.
   An authoritative account of the author-reader relationship in the eighteenth century.
Butt, John, *Fielding*, revised edn. Writers and Their Work No. 57. Longmans, Green, London 1959.
   An excellent brief introduction to Fielding's life and work.
Coley, William B., 'Gide and Fielding '. *Comparative Literature*, Vol. XI, 1959, pp. 1-15.
   An interesting account of Gide's view of Fielding, and of the epic tone of *Tom Jones*.
Compton, Neil (ed.), *Henry Fielding: Tom Jones: A Casebook*. Macmillan, London 1970.
   A useful collection of early and modern criticism.
Crane, R. S., 'The Concept of Plot and the Plot of *Tom Jones*' in R. S. Crane (ed.), *Critics and Criticism: Ancient and Modern*. University of Chicago Press, Chicago 1952, pp. 616-47.
   An original and influential essay.
Ehrenpreis, Irvin, *Fielding: Tom Jones*. Arnold, London 1964.
   The best introduction to *Tom Jones*.
Empson, William, 'Tom Jones' in Ronald Paulson (ed.), *Fielding: A Collection of Critical Essays*. Prentice-Hall, Englewood Cliffs, N.J. 1962, pp. 123-45.
   A spirited and perceptive defence of Fielding and *Tom Jones*.
Ford, Ford Madox, *The English Novel*. Lippincott, London and Philadelphia 1929.
   Includes one of the most extreme attacks on Fielding.
Harrison, Bernard, *Henry Fielding's Tom Jones: The Novelist as Moral Philosopher*. Sussex University Press, London 1975.
   A lively defence of the originality and philosophical respectability of Fielding's moral thought.
Hassall, Anthony J., 'Fielding's Puppet Image'. *Philological Quarterly*, Vol. 53, 1974, pp. 71-83.
Hatfield, Glenn W., *Henry Fielding and the Language of Irony*. University of Chicago Press, Chicago and London 1968.
   Contains a useful chapter on prudence in *Tom Jones*.
Hilles, Frederick W., 'Art and Artifice in *Tom Jones*' in Maynard Mack and Ian Gregor (eds), *Imagined Worlds*. Methuen, London 1968, pp. 91-110.
   An interesting account of the structure of *Tom Jones*.
Hunter, J. Paul, *Occasional Form*. Johns Hopkins University Press, Baltimore and London 1975.
   Includes three interesting chapters on *Tom Jones*.
Hutchens, Eleanor N., *Irony in Tom Jones*. University of Alabama Press 1965.
   Examines some examples of Fielding's irony in detail.
Johnson, Maurice, *Fielding's Art of Fiction*. University of Pennsylvania Press, Philadelphia 1961.
   Four of the chapters examine aspects of *Tom Jones* closely.
Lockwood, Thomas, 'Matter and Reflection in *Tom Jones*'. *ELH*, Vol. 45, 1978, pp. 226-35.

Miller, Henry Knight, 'The "Digressive" Tales in Fielding's *Tom Jones* and the Perspective of Romance'. *Philological Quarterly*, Vol. 54, 1975, pp. 258–74.

—, *Essays on Fielding's Miscellanies: A Commentary on Volume One*. Princeton University Press, Princeton 1961.
Remains the best account of Fielding's thought and art.

—, *Henry Fielding's 'Tom Jones' and the Romance Tradition*. University of Victoria, B.C. 1976.
Traces Fielding's debt to the Romances and offers a persuasive reading of *Tom Jones*.

—, 'Some Functions of Rhetoric in *Tom Jones*'. *Philological Quarterly*, Vol. XLV, 1966, pp. 209–35.
A classic essay on Fielding's rhetoric.

—, 'The Voices of Henry Fielding: Style in *Tom Jones*' in H. K. Miller *et al.* (eds), *The Augustan Milieu*. Clarendon, Oxford 1970, pp. 262–88.

Murry, J. Middleton, 'In Defence of Fielding' in *Unprofessional Essays*. Cape, London 1956, pp. 11–52.
Defends Tom's sexual behaviour.

Osborne, John, *Tom Jones: A Film Script*. Faber, London 1964.

Paulson, Ronald (ed.), *Fielding: A Collection of Critical Essays*. Prentice-Hall, Englewood Cliffs, N.J. 1962.
Includes five essays on *Tom Jones*.

Paulson, Ronald and Lockwood, Thomas (eds), *Henry Fielding: The Critical Heritage*. Routledge, London, Barnes & Noble, New York 1969.
The fullest collection of early criticism. Covers the period 1730 to 1787.

Preston, John, *The Created Self: The Reader's Role in Eighteenth-Century Fiction*. Heinemann, London 1970.
Includes two interesting chapters on *Tom Jones*.

Price, Martin, 'Fielding: The Comedy of Forms' in *To the Palace of Wisdom*. Doubleday, New York 1965, pp. 286–312.
A suggestive and succinct essay on Fielding.

Rawson, C. J., *Henry Fielding and the Augustan Ideal under Stress*. Routledge, London and Boston 1972.
Examines the darker side of Fielding's vision.

—(ed.), *Henry Fielding: A Critical Anthology*. Penguin, Harmondsworth 1973.
Generous collection of criticism from 1730 to 1968.

Sacks, Sheldon, *Fiction and the Shape of Belief*. University of California Press, Berkeley and Los Angeles 1964.
An interesting discussion of the embodiment of Fielding's beliefs in his fiction.

Sherburn, George, 'Fielding's Social Outlook' in James L. Clifford (ed.), *Eighteenth-Century English Literature: Modern Essays in Criticism*. Oxford University Press, New York 1959, pp. 251–73.

Spilka, Mark, 'Fielding and the Epic Impulse'. *Criticism*, Vol. XI, 1969, pp. 68–77.

Williams, Ioan (ed.), *The Criticism of Henry Fielding*. Routledge, London 1970.
Collects Fielding's own criticism.

Wright, Andrew, *Henry Fielding: Mask and Feast*. Chatto & Windus, London 1965.
A perceptive study of the novels.